who is God?

Who Is God?

The Soul's Road Home

Irma Zaleski

Foreword by
Philip Zaleski

New Seeds
Boston
2006

New Seeds Books
An imprint of
Shambhala Publications, Inc.
Horticultural Hall
300 Massachusetts Avenue
Boston, Massachusetts 02115
www.newseedsbooks.com

© 2003 Novalis, Saint Paul University, Ottawa, Canada
Foreword © 2006 by Philip Zaleski

All rights reserved. No part of this book may be reproduced
in any form or by any means, electronic or mechanical, including
photocopying, recording, or by any information storage and retrieval
system, without permission in writing from the publisher.

9   8   7   6   5   4   3   2   1

First New Seeds Edition
Printed in the United States of America

⊗This edition is printed on acid-free paper that meets
the American National Standards Institute z39.48 Standard.
Distributed in the United States by Random House, Inc.,
and in Canada by Random House of Canada Ltd

Library of Congress Cataloging-in-Publication Data
Zaleski, Irma.
Who is God?/Irma Zaleski; foreword by Philip Zaleski.
p. cm.
Originally published: Who is God? Canada: Novalis, 2003.
Includes bibliographical references.
ISBN-13: 978-1-59030-304-7 (alk. paper)
ISBN-10: 1-59030-304-0
1. Mystery.   2. God.   3. Faith.   I. Title.
BT127.5.Z35 2006
242—dc22
2006000683

Contents

Part II: The Vision of Faith

Part III: Conversion of the Heart

Foreword

One of the most haunting passages in the New Testament occurs in the eighth chapter of the Gospel of John, as a group of Pharisees, seeking to trap Jesus in blasphemy, bring to him a woman guilty of adultery and ask whether she should be stoned to death, as the law commanded:

> This they said, tempting him, that they might have to accuse him. But Jesus stooped down, and with his finger wrote on the ground, as though he heard them not. So when they continued asking him, he lifted up himself, and said unto them, He that is without sin among you, let him first cast a stone at her. And again he stooped down, and wrote on the ground. And they which heard it, being convicted by their own conscience, went out one by one, beginning at the eldest, even unto the last: and Jesus was left alone, and the woman standing in the midst. (John 8:6-9, KJV)

The most celebrated part of this passage is undoubtedly Jesus's counsel, commonly phrased as "Let he who is without sin cast the first stone," a teaching of such intense force that it has become a cornerstone of the Christian moral legacy. What catches the eye with almost equal power, however, is the description of Jesus writing on the ground. Immediately, a host of questions arise: Did Jesus write in sand, dirt, clay, or mud? Did he use his finger, a stick, a straw? In what language did he write? Aramaic? Hebrew? The tongue of heaven? And above all, *what did he write?* Nearly two thousand years of New Testament study have brought us no closer to answering these questions; Jesus's actions remain enveloped in mystery. Nor is this atypical; the New Testament teems with enigmatic events and pronouncements, including the ebb and flow of Jesus's powers, the parables and the "I am" sayings, the raising of Lazarus, the Transfiguration, the Resurrection itself. The Gospel, it may be fairly said, is awash in mystery.

These biblical episodes point also to another, closely related set of mysteries: those involving the nature of faith, the meaning of love, the being of God. These are the themes addressed in the slim yet substantial volume you hold in your hands. Irma Zaleski (to whom, despite the coincidence of surnames, the present writer is not related) has spent over half a century pondering and exploring the pathways of faith, and here she presents, with warmth, gentleness, and considerable wisdom, the fruits of her labors. Opening ourselves to mystery is, Zaleski says, the first step toward spiritual maturity, the beginning of the great personal transformation required of every human being, a process that ends only when we have become "the 'true self' that we were created to be." Among the greatest of these spiritual mysteries are the palpable sense of divine presence that comes upon us when we attend to God with all our being, the awareness that this presence is identical to love, and the realization that sharing in this love is the only way to know God ("He that loveth not knoweth not God, for God is love," 1 John 4:8).

Around these core ideas press a number of others, which often venture into paradox or enigma: that we know God by "unknowing," by surrendering the certainties cherished by our egos; that faith is not blind acceptance of unproven facts but a form of love, a willingness to embrace God as a living reality; that dogmas are not dry husks of belief but doorways into enlightenment; that doubt can be a useful tool in the search for truth, as well as a deadly poison; that the true home of the mind is in the heart. None of these ideas, as Zaleski says, are original with her; her role is to offer a contemporary expression of traditional Christian teachings. These ideas may appear new, however, to those unfamiliar with the Church's long history of fostering the inner life, to those who mistakenly believe that Christianity, unlike, say, Buddhism, is a religion of externals. In truth, Buddhism is as rich in liturgy and art as Christianity, and Christianity cultivates as keen a sense of spiritual investigation as Buddhism. This is not to say that these two religions or any two spiritual paths are equivalent; Zaleski holds her ground on this matter, explaining that while all religions reveal truth, for Christians Jesus is and must be the perfect expression of Truth. She writes as an orthodox Christian, deeply saturated with the finest elements of her tradition.

Nonetheless, Zaleski presents ideas in a way that embraces the longings of people of every creed and of none. Her meditations on silence, repentance, tolerance, and compassion speak to us all. Her concerns are universal: how to live honestly, fruitfully, cherishing what is beautiful and good; in a word, how to love. She offers advice on venerable Christian practices—the Jesus Prayer, remembrance of the presence of God, mindful obedience—that lead toward this goal. The ultimate aim of Christianity, she tells us, is divinization, active participation in the divine self-giving love of the Trinity. Zaleski quotes an acquaintance of hers who describes our struggles toward that culminating love—a work that consists largely of not standing in the way of God's grace—as "living the life of heaven while still on earth."

This is about as good a definition of the Christian project as one can find. *Who Is God?* is filled with such spiritual gems, and, as such, is a welcome addition to the library of spiritual works that present the ancient wisdom of the Christian tradition to modern hearts and minds.

Philip Zaleski

Philip Zaleski is editor of the Best American Spiritual Writing series and author, with his wife Carol Zaleski, of *Prayer: A History* (Houghton Mifflin, 2005).

Introduction

Many years ago, I heard a story about an American Zen master, a woman who had become a Buddhist as a young adult. Her relatives were shocked and dismayed and could not reconcile themselves with her decision. They kept asking her, "Do you at least believe in God?" One day, as they asked her this question yet again, she became exasperated and exclaimed: "And who is God?"

When I first heard this story, I thought it was a good example of the way Zen masters often deal with their disciples' metaphysical questions: by refusing to answer such questions and instead redirecting their disciples' attention to another, more fundamental problem or *koan*. The disciples are expected to work on the problem until they find the answer to it by themselves or, more likely, until they realize that the problem cannot be solved by thinking: that it lies *beyond* thought.

I was a little irritated by the Zen master's answer as well, for it could also imply that those of us who claim to believe in God do not really know what we are talking about. But I soon became convinced that all of us "believers" would do well to ask ourselves the same question very seriously at least once in our lives. It is important to admit that, if we are honest with ourselves, we do not really know how to answer this question in a way that would satisfy our own minds, let alone a Zen master. We do not know who God is. We cannot prove God's existence or explain God in words.

It seems very easy, especially for us in the West, to forget that, in this life at least, God—the Ultimate Reality, the Source of all being—is a Mystery that human reason cannot penetrate nor words express. While we are on earth, we can only see God "as in a mirror darkly." (1 Corinthians 13:12) We cannot understand or "solve" this Mystery, we can only open ourselves to it and learn to receive it, not with our minds but at the core of our being: with our hearts.

To say "I don't know" about the things that matter to us most is very frightening. It requires a patient, laborious, unceasing effort to let go of our illusions of wisdom and our pretenses of being knowledge-able about things we cannot know. It means being prepared to stand silent and unknowing before the Mystery of God and to place all our trust in his mercy and love. The knowledge of God to which we are called is not achieved through study and thought, but is a vision given to the heart.

This is a book of reflections on this immense Mystery of God: on the mystery of faith that is also a mystery of love; on opening our small, finite being to the infinite being of God; on remembering him always and learning to live in his presence. It is also a book of reflections on the path of transformation that we must follow in order to become the true images, or *icons*, of God that we have been created to be; on the difficulties we may have to face on the way; on the doubts that may torment us; but also on the joy the journey will bring us. For the Presence we search for is not only the final goal of our journey, but also our daily experience: our own true life, the Kingdom of God growing within our hearts.

As I look back on the many years of my own search, of endless failures and wrong turnings and of even more endless mercy and grace, I begin to realize the uniqueness of the path to which each one of us has been called. We can help and encourage each other, we can share what we have learned with each other, but we cannot find the path or walk it for anyone else.

Irma Zaleski

Part I

The Mystery of God

The Heart of Religion

At the source of every religious tradition and every spiritual path lies a conviction that there is more to existence than life as we know it on earth; that the universe is penetrated and filled with another, greater Reality; that at the core of creation burns a profound Mystery that cannot be grasped by human reason but can be revealed and experienced. The purpose of our life on earth, and the goal of all religion, is to open ourselves to this Mystery and be transformed by it into a new mode of being, to become the "true self" that we were created to be.

This vision of the world filled with the light of the Mystery lies also at the heart of Christianity. This vision is not yet "revealed religion" but the mind's first necessary step towards it — the soil on which the seed of revealed faith can be cast. Without this soil, no religious conviction could take root. It would be like the seed cast on barren rock in Christ's parable. It could not bear fruit.

The heart of religion — and the beginning of faith — is not a system of doctrine or moral law, but an attitude of mind and a way of life open to the love of what Rudolf Otto called the "The Holy."[1] It is a conviction that, in spite of the suffering and evil that so often appear to overwhelm the world, at the centre of reality lies not the darkness of *absence*, but a great mystery of *presence and love*. The world is filled with a Presence for which we may have no name, whose existence we cannot prove, but which we can recognize, experience and marvel at.

I once heard the English poet Christopher Dawson say that poetry is "the language in which man explores his amazement." The same can surely be said of all great art and literature, all great science and philosophy. But, above all, the same can be — and must be — said about religion.

We cannot become truly religious, truly open to the Mystery of God, until we are able to be amazed at the mystery of existence — the mystery of the universe, but also of ourselves. Truly religious people are those who "have eyes to see" the whole of created reality aflame with the glory and holiness of God and who recognize in the Mystery of the Divine Presence the fundamental answer to the question of the purpose and meaning of existence.

The Mysteriousness
of Things

T he sense of amazement and mystery seems to be a natural (although often misunderstood) gift belonging to every human being. Most children whose childhood has not been torn away from them by tragedy or evil seem to possess it. Children are aware of the mysteriousness of things. They love stories of magic and adventure in worlds that are not visible to their eyes but that are still very real to them. They are conscious of mystery — a "presence" — hiding behind everything they see, everything they touch or hear.

Children do not think much about this "presence." They do not call it "God" — they do not tend to have a name for it at all. They simply take it for granted; it is an added dimension to their everyday reality. Children seem to be able to experience the visible world not as a closed-off, self-contained universe, but as a window or a door to a mysterious, sometimes glorious, sometimes terrifying, but always utterly fascinating reality just beyond.

It would be a great, even a tragic mistake to dismiss children's sense of mystery, and their delight in it, as unimportant. It might do them irreparable harm to discourage or even suppress it, which happens all too often. Their sense of mystery must be respected, guided and protected because it is their first step on the path of spiritual life. It is their first taste of the Holy, their preparation for the gift of faith.[2]

Most of us, when we grow up, lose this natural contact with the mystery. We leave it behind, as we leave behind other "childish" things. We learn to mistrust any experience of a reality that cannot be seen or touched, that cannot be grasped by thought or expressed in words. Perhaps we fear that the mystery, if we open ourselves to it, might destroy our adult sense of boundaries, tear down our defenses and expose us to a universe too vast and unfriendly for our small, vulnerable self. Like Adam and Eve, when we hear God walking in the garden, we hide from him, afraid. Thus, we live in a flat, reasonable world from which mystery and wonder seem to have disappeared forever and in which religious faith seems an aberration, an escape from reality, or just plain foolishness.

Yet, one day, unexpected and unhoped for, the world we had thought irretrievably lost may be returned to us. In a moment of insight—a sudden opening of the heart—we may glimpse again the mysterious reality we took for granted as children. We may again experience its wonder and delight. Now, however, we discover that the mystery in whose presence we again find ourselves is infinitely more mysterious than the "magic" of childhood and infinitely more beautiful than anything we can see or imagine in this life. The mystery, we realize, is the Mystery of the Divine Presence filling the whole universe with its power and light.

The Meaning of Mystery

Sometimes we shy away from the word "mystery" because we hear it used so often in ways that may have obscured its original meaning. We call a fictitious detective story a mystery; we talk about mysterious events, a mysterious person, or someone's mysterious past. The word "mystery," like many other great and important words, has been trivialized. Its original meaning, however, points to a fundamental aspect of reality; no other word in our language can replace it.

"Mystery" comes from the Greek word *mysterion*, which refers to the secret rites of initiation of ancient esoteric religions. During these rites, it was assumed, "true knowledge" about the nature of the universe and the meaning of existence was passed on to those judged ready to receive it. The etymology of the word is significant, for the Greek verb from which it was derived originally meant "to close eyes or lips." Thus, it implies that those who wish to find true wisdom—those who want to find and possess the Truth—must close their physical senses, must go *beyond* knowledge based on their rational, "thinking" minds, and open the *eyes of their hearts*, their inner understanding or insight.

(Greek) noun – mind beyond the
(noun) mind

The ancient and powerful image of a blind prophet or sage or a "wise fool" can help us understand the way we must approach the Mystery of God. Both are well known in the literature and sacred scriptures of many religions.

They are also well known in Christianity. The "mysteries of the kingdom," Christ said, were not open to those "who have eyes but they do not see; who have ears but they do not hear." (Matthew 13:11, 13) It is when we think we see what we cannot see that we are truly blind. When St. Paul said that "God made the wisdom of the world foolish" (1 Corinthians 1:20), he pointed to the same paradox. It is when we delude ourselves that we can see the Mystery of God with our human eyes, or grasp it with our human minds, that we are most foolish. We are, to use a wonderfully descriptive Zen image, like a mosquito trying to bite its way through a metal mountain.

Yet to the world it appears otherwise. In many ways, our culture resembles the mosquito busy at its impossible task. Our culture considers rational knowledge the highest, the most legitimate and, often, the only way to truth. It tends to reduce all existential or metaphysical questions into mere problems to be examined by the mind and, eventually, to be solved by science or technology, by some super-computer, perhaps. All questions that cannot be thus solved — that are perceived as not having rational solutions — are therefore considered nonsensical and absurd.

The Wise Fool

I t is therefore not surprising that the world we live in is not always comfortable with people who claim that they "see" what the majority cannot see, or with those who admit to a belief in a mystery whose existence they cannot prove or explain in rational terms. To most contemporary men and women, such an attitude seems to belong to an irrational fanatic or a fool lost in an illusion, to those who "see" what is not there—as in Hans Christian Andersen's tale of "The Emperor's New Clothes."

Very few of us are able to remain indifferent to our society's ideas and assumptions. Above all else, we fear being despised and considered foolish in a world where foolishness is immeasurably more shameful than sinfulness, and being knowledgeable is much more important than being loving or good. To be a fool means to perceive reality in a manner that to most people seems absurd, even insane; to embrace a way of life that the world views as irrational and based on *un-reason*. To be a fool is to be alone—outside the safety of common perceptions and values, outside the culture in which we live, work and find our proper place. Fools make people uneasy; they are an embarrassment to their family and friends.

Our alienation is perhaps even more fundamental than that. We often find ourselves with our own hearts and minds divided: estranged not only from the ways of thought and perception that our culture assumes to be the only rational ones, but also from parts of ourselves. We question the wisdom and the values of the world but we also question ourselves; we mistrust our own belief in anything that cannot be understood, touched or seen, because we cannot help associating it with irrationality — denial of the mind — which has so often wreaked havoc on and brought misery to the world.

We may feel embarrassed about our religious beliefs. We may want to play them down, to make them appear, even to ourselves, as reasonable and free of mystery. We may try to make God fit into categories acceptable to our thinking minds, to explain God in terms borrowed from psychology, anthropology, even physics. We may want to make God into an idea or a concept that can be inserted in some way into a rational, scientific universe. We may want to make him into an "archetype," a "cosmic principle," a "force" or, according to a more recent theory, a "design."

Yet it is not possible to make God "reasonable" or to fit God into any categories of science or thought. Science and rational inquiry, however essential, exciting and awe-inspiring they are to the human mind, are ultimately irrelevant to our experience of God;

they cannot judge the truth of religion, because the Truth religion seeks is infinite and thus beyond thought. To find God we must be willing to accept and carry the burden — and the embarrassment — of being "fools."

True Wisdom

The foolishness that we are speaking about here, the foolishness that is "wiser than the wisdom of the world" (1 Corinthians 1:25)—like any other spiritual gift—has many pitfalls. One of the most dangerous, because it is so difficult for us to discern in ourselves, is spiritual pride. We may come to believe that, however foolish and naive we may appear in the eyes of the world, we are not foolish at all; we *do* know something that the wise of this world do not know and therefore are wiser than they.

We may imagine that we have been given some superior knowledge or superior spiritual powers; we may convince ourselves that we have had a special revelation, that we can foresee the future of the world, that we have come to understand the mind of God! We may even fall into the most dangerous illusion of all and believe that we are *better,* holier than others, that we are "chosen of God." And thus, we may end up worse off than we began. We may find ourselves in the condition that the Greek philosopher Socrates called *double ignorance*—the foolishness of those who think they know what they do not know.

The wisdom of those who enter the kingdom of

Heaven does not mean pretending to be fools when, in their heart of hearts, they are convinced that they are not. Neither does it mean embracing some kind of bizarre behaviour, becoming religious "hippies" or rebels, or taking up the role of protesters against the rest of humankind. True fools, the "Holy Fools," do not protest or rebel against anything. They do not think that they know better, that they are wiser or better than others. True fools know that, before the face of God, they are indeed foolish, indeed sinners; they have no claim to any special status at all. They know that accepting this reality of the human condition is the first, essential step on the way to wisdom.

The goal of every true religious path is not to make us appear wise and thus to gain the respect and praise of others. The goal of religion is to call us out of our small, frightened self, to make us aware of our finiteness and the poverty of our ordinary thinking mind. Religion does not do away with our ordinary mind—or any aspect of our ordinary human reality. Rather, it stretches it, transforms it and opens it to the Divine Reality. It does not present us with a solution to the Mystery, but summons us to approach it as Moses approached the burning bush in the desert: with face covered, barefoot and trembling in awe.

The Burning Bush

⌒

The story of the burning bush (Exodus 3) captures with amazing clarity the very essence of human encounter with the Mystery of God. It shows us a man walking across the desert, a shepherd minding his flocks: an ordinary moment in time. Suddenly, the man sees flames—a bush is on fire. Strange, he thinks, but not frightening or extraordinary. But when he looks at it again, he is amazed to see that the bush is not being consumed by the fire! That is indeed strange, he realizes. "I must go and look at this remarkable sight," he says to himself, puzzled but still unafraid. "I must see why the bush is not burned." This seems a sensible, human reaction to a very unusual situation: a problem to be looked at, investigated and solved.

At this point, the veil of the ordinary is torn aside and the Mystery enters human reality. At the heart of the visible, the Invisible burns. "Moses! Moses!" God calls from the bush, "Come no nearer! Remove the sandals from your feet, for the place where you stand is holy ground." Moses hides his face and bows to the ground, for he knows that to gaze at the blazing Holiness of God unveiled would blind his earthly eyes and overwhelm his mind. He would be wrenched from the ordinary forever.

But the ordinary is not destroyed in this encounter with God. Moses is still Moses: he does not lose his mind. He hears, he answers, he remembers his old fear of Pharaoh's vengeance, he argues with God, he asks for guarantees and proof. God makes himself "ordinary" so that Moses may understand him and yet not be consumed. Man and God talk like individuals, like friends.

Of course, Moses' understanding of the ordinary differed greatly from ours. Mystery was still part of his world. He had no doubts that the Reality that confronted him from the burning bush was God. He had no doubt about God's Holiness or Power. He covered his eyes not because he thought what he saw before him was an illusion, but because he knew it was real, although too bright for him to see. Moses had not lost the capacity to accept the Invisible that most people today experience only as children.

And yet, we must not exaggerate Moses' faith or humility. As the story continues, we see that the mind of Moses was not that different from ours after all. He was still doubtful, he was still afraid, he still wanted answers and guarantees. In the midst of his encounter with the Mystery, having seen the burning fire of the Presence and having heard

God's voice, he insists that God explain himself; he questions God's command that Moses lead his people and even asks that he, a human being, should be told the *Name of God*.

The Name of God

The mysterious answer God gave to Moses, the YHWH of the Hebrew text, has been debated by both Hebrew and Christian scholars for centuries.[3]

The debates were very important to the development of Western thought. Yet it is essential to realize that they in no way dispelled or even diminished the Mystery of God, or made it more comprehensible to our rational minds. All the arguments and writings of scholars cannot penetrate its heart, as the greatest theologians—the truly wise—have always recognized. For, as the Greek Fathers—the early teachers of the Christian Tradition—had warned, "a God who is comprehensible is not God"[4] should never be far from our minds.

There is still another important point to reflect on. Most traditional cultures, and certainly the Hebrews, believed the name of a person to be the key to his or her true identity. Thus, revealing one's true name to others would grant them power over one's soul, life and death. But no human being could ever hold such power over God. We should not, therefore, assume that God intended to reveal the whole mystery of his Name to Moses—God knew Moses could not survive such a revelation—but only to let him see the "back" of it: a glimpse. (Exodus 33:18-23) As one of the early Fathers, St. Gregory of Nyssa, said in the fourth century, "God's name is not to be known, but to be wondered at."[5]

For this reason, the words God speaks to Moses immediately after he gives him his "I Am" answer are very significant. He says, "Thus you shall say to the Israelites: The Lord God of your fathers, the God of Abraham, of Isaac and of Jacob has sent me to you." And he adds, "*This is my name forever*, this is my title for all generations." It seems clear that here God is not speaking of who God is *in himself*, but rather of who he is in relationship *to us*. It is the Name we learn not in courses on philosophy or theology but only in our life with God.

God is telling Moses that he can be known only as he reveals himself in our human reality: in the events of our lives, in history, in ordinary time. Above all, God reveals himself in a personal encounter, in a relationship of love. We must learn to recognize the Divine Presence, hear God's voice and believe. This means *trusting* in God, whose existence we cannot prove, whose being we cannot comprehend, whose "true name" we cannot know, but whom we can meet and whose presence we can experience and recognize.

Theophany

The story of Moses' encounter with God is a story of a *theophany*—a *shining forth* of the light of God into our ordinary, human reality. It is not a story of a human mind achieving some supernatural, esoteric knowledge of the Mystery of God, but a story of the light of the Divine Presence penetrating the darkness of our understanding.

In other words, theophany—often called "epiphany" in the West—is not an "ascent" of our human minds to the Divine Presence, but a *descent*: it is God descending and revealing himself to us. Theophany, in the biblical tradition, is a sacred event—an encounter—always initiated by God. It is an event that cannot be understood but can be experienced and marvelled at.

It is true that there have always been some who interpreted many aspects of Christian religion—its rites, its sacraments, its spiritual teaching—in an esoteric way. From that perspective, the Gospels themselves, especially the Gospel of John, may be viewed as written in symbols, in a kind of secret code that can be penetrated only by a few. Most Christians, however—and the official teaching of both the Catholic and the Orthodox Church—have held to the belief that the Gospels teach a wisdom and point to a spiritual path that is open to all. This path is not easy — *never* easy — but is very simple. We become wise, and holy, not by a path of higher knowledge but, as we have said already, by the "foolishness" of faith.

The wisdom God gives to those who love and seek him is very ordinary: it opens the eyes of our hearts to the Mystery of Divine Presence in the everyday human reality. This is why, the saints assure us, when we finally realize the limitations of our finite mind, we are not filled with anxiety or despair but only with *joy*. This joy stems from the realization that God is so much greater and more wonderful than anything our small minds could ever imagine or prove. It is the joy of stepping out beyond the limits of our understanding, beyond ourselves, and into the Presence of God. As Mother Maria Gysi once wrote in a short essay on the Trinity,

> I think it is the very greatest help for us . . . to know that there is something absolutely beyond us, a Mystery of love . . . of which our most eloquent witness is deep silence of adoration, where mind and will are set at rest on a subject beyond their grasp . . . in the peace and joy of the presence of the Perfect.[6]

All religious traditions must have such "theophanies," moments of the Divine breaking through.

An epiphany does not need to be a momentous event, however. Most of us have our own small theophanies: sudden moments of insight, joy or love when our ordinary, earthly reality suddenly becomes numinous, when it glows with the light of the Divine Presence and God speaks to us from a "burning bush." We, like Moses, can only meet God, in the words of an anonymous medieval writer, in a "cloud of unknowing"—not in the light of reason, but in the *unknowing of faith*.

Unknowing

The notion of faith as "unknowing" may seem surprising, even shocking to us at first, because it appears to contradict the fundamental belief of both Hebrew and Christian traditions, as well as of all other great religions, that knowledge of the truth is the path to God. The Bible insists that in order to be "righteous," and to have eternal life, we must know God. True religion does not demand sacrifices and burnt offerings, but *love and knowledge of God.* (Hosea 6:6) Christ himself sanctioned this understanding of faith when he said that "eternal life is to know God and the One he has sent." (John 17:3)

The same conviction is evident in the whole of the New Testament and in the Christian teaching since apostolic times. Faith opens the eyes of our heart to the *knowledge* of God (Ephesians 1:17-18); it helps us to understand the mystery of reality. "I believe in order to understand; and I understand, the better to believe," St. Augustine wrote in the fifth century.[7] "Faith *seeks understanding,*" as St. Anselm put it in the twelfth.[8] How, then, is it possible to say that we cannot know God?

Our confusion is frequently due, at least partly, to a misunderstanding of the meaning of certain key words such as "knowledge," "mind" or "faith" as they were used in Hebrew and Greek, the languages in which our religious tradition was first expressed. The English word "knowledge" may be especially misleading, for it can have several different meanings — often expressed in different words in the original languages — and it is not always clear which meaning is intended. Thus we say that we "know" how to play music or tennis, when we mean that we have a certain acquired skill or ability in that area. We say we know a historical fact, or a chemical formula, or the way to a place, when we have learned something from experience or through science. We say that we know that a lemon is sour, because we have tasted it and remember what it tasted like.

None of the above kinds of "knowing" can be applied to God, because they are either based on sensory experience or are a product of scientific inquiry or rational thought; neither sense experience, nor science, nor rational thought can comprehend God.

There is, however, yet another sense of the word "knowledge" that is closer to the intended meaning of the original Hebrew and Greek texts when applied to God. The biblical word we translate as "knowing" in relation to God is more appropriately translated as getting to know, in the sense of getting to know a person, especially someone we love. Thus, the Bible talks about a man "knowing" a woman, not only in the sense of their physical union, but also in the sense of their total relationship of love.

In the same way, in the biblical tradition, when we talk about the "knowledge of God" we do not mean knowledge derived from study or arrived at through rational thought, but knowledge found in a personal relationship with God: in an encounter of love. As *The Cloud of Unknowing* says,

> Through grace, a man can have great knowledge of all other creatures and their works, and even of the works of God Himself and can think of them all. But of God Himself no man can think. . . . *Because he can well be loved, but not thought of.*[9]

Knowledge of God is the *knowledge of love.*

Knowledge of Love

If we find it difficult to understand this "knowledge of love," it may be because we think of love mainly in terms of emotion or of an overwhelming personal need. We think we are "in love" when we desperately need another person, when we consider others indispensable to our happiness, even our life.

But such "love" is not true love. It is a form of *self-love*: it is mainly concerned with our own needs and happiness. Emotion and need are often the beginning of love; they are the mechanisms that compel us to search for love and open ourselves to it. True love, however, is not based on emotion or need but on willingness to place the good and the needs of another above our own. True love — mature love — is the choice to go out of ourselves and to be truly *present* to another, truly *aware* of another. It is a total, non-judgmental acceptance of another.

When we love, we become aware of others in a way that is much deeper than just being aware of their physical presence. We recognize them as persons, we recognize their uniqueness, their beauty, their power to evoke our love. Love is a relationship between persons. Only a person can love, for only a person can be aware of another as if of oneself and thus *love another as oneself.*

We know those we love in a way that no other way of knowing can approach. We know them from inside, from our inner being, from the heart. We do not judge them, we do not want to change them, we accept them and love them as they are. Such love makes it possible for us to open ourselves to certain people, to believe in them and to trust them in a way we cannot know and trust others, even those we may have known for a much longer time and about whom we may have more information, more facts.

On the other hand, it is also true, and very significant, that when we are asked to describe those we love to others, or even when we try to think about them, we feel unable to put our knowledge into words. We can talk about their character, appearance or behaviour, but we find no words that adequately express what they really are to us, how we see them with the eyes of love. It often seems to us that the more we love, the less we can say about the person we love. The more we love someone, the more of a *mystery* that person seems to become for us. The "knowing" of love is not only beyond words, it is also beyond understanding.

If this is true of human love, how much more true it must be of the love of God! The Mystery of

God is infinitely bigger than anything our thinking minds can understand or express. Whatever we can understand about God is only a drop in the sea of our unknowing. Or, to use an image St. Augustine used, when we try to comprehend God or explain him in words, we are like children trying to empty the ocean of its water by scooping it into a little pond they made on the shore.

Religious teachers in every age and from every tradition realized this truth. Words and thoughts, as a Zen saying puts it, are only "fingers pointing at the moon." They can direct us to the Mystery, they can point it out to us, but they cannot make us see it, understand it or express it. Truth of God, like love, is *inexpressible*.

Inexpressible Truth

The Fathers of the Church, as we have already seen, insisted that a god who can be "named" is not God. This is why they believed that God can best be approached in silence. In *Sayings of the Desert Fathers*, we find a wonderful story that illustrates this conviction:

> When Abba Zacharias was on the point of dying, Abba Moses asked him, "What do you see?" But Abba Zacharias replied, "Is it not better to say nothing, Father?" "Yes, my son," said Abba Moses, "it is better to hold your peace."[10]

St. Isaac the Syrian expressed the same truth when he said that "speech is the organ of the present world, silence is the mystery of the world to come."[11] Words and concepts can only point to the Mystery of God; they cannot express it, explain it or prove that it exists.

Silence before God does not mean that we should never talk about God. Language is a tool that, however imperfect, we must use, for there is no other way to communicate with each other or even, most of the time, with God. In all theistic religious traditions (traditions that believe in a personal God) it is taken for granted that God sometimes "talks" to human beings. When he does, it is their sacred obligation to pass the divine words to others (cf. Jeremiah 20:9). Scriptures are sacred precisely because they are believed to be inspired words of God.

This conviction that God sometimes "talks" to human beings has been especially evident in Christianity because of its belief that God's own Word—the full revelation of his Being—was made flesh in the Person of Christ. Through the Incarnation, everything human has been raised to an immensely greater dignity; it acquired a potential and a significance we could not have imagined before. Through the Incarnation, human words became capable of bearing the Mystery of God: not of fully expressing or explaining it, but *bearing* it—making it present—in a way that icons bear the sacred images they "re-present."

The words of the Bible, and in a special way of the Gospels, can therefore be said to be *inspired*—anointed with the Spirit. They are, we might say, "sacramental": they make God present to us, they have the power to move our hearts and open them to faith. We do not just read about Christ in the Gospels, we meet him. This is why we venerate the Gospels, we stand when they are read, we bow before the book that contains them, we kiss it and keep it in a place of honour. The same power, although in a smaller measure, has been given to the words used in the ancient liturgies, hymns and prayers of the Church.

Thus we must use words, but we must use them "austerely," as Mother Maria Gysi used to say. We must be aware of their limitations and humble before the unknowable Reality to which they point. We must try to speak—or write—as clearly and simply as we can. We must say "yes" when we mean "yes" and "no" when we mean "no." We must speak the truth or, at least, we must try, for such austerity is excruciatingly difficult for most of us.

What We Truly Mean

Anthony Bloom, the Russian Orthodox Metropolitan of Sourozh, once told me that in order to learn how to pray, *I must never say one word to God that I do not truly mean*. I was quite shocked, I remember, even a little frightened, when this statement began to sink in. "But how can I do that?" I said. "I do not often even *know* what I truly mean!" "Well," he replied, "you had better practise it!"

I don't think I realized at that moment the significance of his words — not only for the way we pray, but for the way we must approach the Truth of God. For if it is true that we must never say even one word that we do not truly mean *to* God, it must also be true that we must never say — or write — one word that we do not truly mean *about* God. We must only speak of what we really believe, what we have experienced and are ready to carry out in our own lives.

This kind of truth requires a form of discipline — a kind of austerity — that is very difficult for most of us. We talk so much, we fill the ears of our friends, or the pages of our books, with what we claim to be our own precious thoughts and ideas. In reality, however, we often just repeat other people's words and opinions, without even asking ourselves whether we know what they really mean. We say what is expected of us and express beliefs that we are not even sure we actually hold. No wonder, then, that we may end up not knowing what we "truly mean."

We do not always realize that this is a form of *lying*, all the more dangerous because we are usually unaware of it. We lie — we say what we do not truly mean — usually because we are afraid of being wrong, of offending other people, of being thought a heretic or a fool. Sometimes we even lie to God. We fear that God might be angry with us if we tell him what we really think; God may dislike and reject us, or even send us to hell! We lie, in other words, because we do not trust ourselves, we do not trust others and, above all, we do not trust God. And how, we might ask ourselves, could we be able to know that, unless the truth, although unavailable to our thinking minds, had been, in some fundamental way, implanted in our hearts?

Yet, as we struggle with our fear, as we try — and most often fail — to say only what we are convinced is true, we begin to see a little light guiding us on the way. We realize that, although we do not always know what we truly mean before we say it, we nearly always seem to know what we do not truly mean — what is *not* true — after we have said it.

There seems to be a deep sense of truth within us, too deep, perhaps, to reach with our conscious mind. Yet it is always there, a treasure to be discovered. It is as if we had a tuning fork built deep into our souls that lets us know whenever we are off-key, whenever we are not in harmony with ourselves. If we practice listening to this inner sound, it will become easier and easier to recognize the first false note we make. When this happens, we will learn to let go of it and try to listen again. It is in that willingness to let go, to listen again and again, that we learn austerity of speech.

Austerity of Thought

Austerity of truth does not only mean austerity of speech, it also means austerity of *thought*. We cannot learn to speak austerely unless we also learn to think austerely. This does not mean that we must stop thinking about God any more than it means that we must stop speaking about him or that we must become simple-minded and ignorant. Catherine Doherty[12] often said that in order to know God "we must fold the wings of our intellect." "But," she would always add, "in order to fold them we must have opened them first!" The "unknowing of faith" is not an excuse for not thinking; rather, it helps us decide when to stop thinking—when the knowledge we seek cannot be reached by thought.

A well-known story about St. Thomas Aquinas, the great medieval theologian, illustrates this truth. It is said that when St. Thomas was already an old man, he had an experience of God that made him realize that everything he had ever said or written about God was only "hay," and that he himself was indeed just a "Dumb Ox," as his fellow students apparently called him when he was young.

This story is usually viewed as an example of the true wisdom that St. Thomas reached in his old age.

We should not, however, imagine that St. Thomas must have also reached the conclusion that the many years he had spent thinking and writing about God had been a waste of time, or that he would have become truly wise sooner had he refrained from thinking and writing altogether.

He must have understood better than most of us that we do not really begin to open ourselves to the grace of true wisdom until we try, perhaps for many years, to be wise by our own efforts. Most of us are unable to "fold the wings of our intellect" and be still before the Mystery until we have exhausted ourselves with trying and failing to solve it. It is only at this point of weariness and discouragement with ourselves that true austerity—and true humility—begin.

We become humble and truly wise not when we refuse to think and remain ignorant and "dumb," but when we finally learn to accept the cross of our finiteness; when we learn how to become silent before the Mystery; when we place our trust not in our own thinking or understanding, but only in the holiness and wisdom of God.

The Apophatic Way

This austere way of approaching the Mystery of God through unknowing and love, although often forgotten, is fundamental to Christianity. It was taught by many of the early Fathers and is still practised in the Orthodox Church, where it is referred to as the *apophatic* way, or "the way of negation." Our thinking cannot grasp God, and our words cannot express or define him, but they can point out to us what he is *not*. They lead us to a glimpse of what is true by opening our eyes to what is not true.

Thus, we can say that he is "infinite," not because we know or can imagine what "infinity" is, but because we know that God cannot be finite — limited — and be God. In the same way, we can say that he is infinitely "good," not because we can understand what infinite goodness might mean, but because to say that God is not good would be absurd. We can say that he is eternal, because to suppose that God could die would make no sense at all. In other words, "unknowing of faith" is a kind of *mirror image* of knowing, as St. Paul seemed to imply. (1 Corinthians 13:12)

A story told about St. Anthony the Great expresses this truth. Anthony was the first and perhaps the greatest of the Desert Fathers, the monks who, in the third and fourth centuries of our era, tried to search for God in the silence and austerity of the Egyptian desert.

> One day some monks came to see Abba Anthony. Wanting to test them, the old man suggested a text from the Scriptures and asked them what it meant. Each gave his opinion as he was able. But to each one the old man said, "You have not understood it." Last of all, he said to Abba Joseph, "How would you explain it?" But he replied, "I do not know." Then Abba Anthony said, "Indeed, Abba Joseph has found the way, for he said, *I do not know*."[13]

The austerity of the apophatic way demands a kind of poverty—a kind of death—that may be very difficult for us to accept. It demands that we leave behind the safety of rational thinking and step out into what seems to be a darkness beyond: a darkness through which our senses or our minds cannot guide us, but which we are called to explore. We can never finish exploring it, we can never come to the end of it, because the Mystery we are seeking is infinite, inexhaustible: it has no limit or end. We can never fully solve it, we can never fully possess it, we can never stop and say, "It is enough, now I know it all." As St. Irenaeus of Lyons expressed it, "God will always have something more to teach man, and man will always have something more to learn from God."[14]

When we say that we cannot know God, or that the way to God lies in unknowing, we do not mean that the way can never be found, that we must forever be strangers and exiles from God's presence. We mean that the way of faith lies beyond words and beyond thought. It lies deep at the centre of our being, in our heart. Knowing God is a matter of the heart, rather than of the head.

The Heart-Mind

The heart we mean here is not our physical heart, nor the heart as the symbol and centre of our *emotional* life, as we often think of it now, but the heart as it is understood in most religious traditions: the spiritual centre of our being and an organ of all true knowledge and wisdom. It is also what some spiritual teachers call our "true mind."

Our contemporary Western understanding of the mind tends to be very narrow. Just as we identify all knowledge with rational knowledge, we identify the mind with the head, with thinking. In the past, however, the mind was—and in all religious cultures still is—understood in a much wider and more inclusive way. The mind was seen to possess not only the powers of "just thinking," as Zen masters expressed it—that is, thinking based on logical argument or scientific proof—but also the powers of insight and contemplation, especially the power to seek and love Truth. Our word "philosopher"—which means "lover of wisdom" in Greek—still reflects this understanding of the mind.

From that perspective, it is the power of the mind to recognize, contemplate and love spiritual truth that is its highest and most important function.

Divine Truth exists independently of the mind: it exists whether the mind knows it or not. Truth can, however, reveal itself to the mind willing to search for it and to embrace it with all its strength. The mind can recognize Truth — although still only in glimpses — through the knowledge of love.

It is significant that for the ancients, including the early Christians, the mind was not located in the head, as it is for us, but in the *heart*, the organ of true knowledge as well as of the whole inner life. Our ancestors thought in their hearts, prayed in their hearts, loved, sorrowed and rejoiced in their hearts. They also knew God in their hearts (cf. Psalm 15). Thus, in the early Christian tradition, and in the Orthodox East even now, the Greek word *nous* can be taken to mean either "mind" or "heart." In both cases the mind in its fullest sense — *the heart-mind* — is meant.

This understanding of the mind as an organ not only of intelligence and rational thought but also of contemplation and love is fundamental to all great religious traditions. True religion does not despise the mind, does not minimize its importance but, on the contrary, invests the mind with a dignity that is even greater than rational thought could ever accord to it.

This is perhaps especially the case in the Christian tradition, which sees the mind or the heart purified by faith and love as the true image, the *icon*, of the mind of the Man-God, Christ. In Christian teaching, this "heart-mind" is understood as the deepest part of our being: the existential *core* of our whole personhood, the centre that draws it all together. It is there that God makes himself present to us and opens us to his love.

Presence

As we have already said, the most fundamental meaning of love—and its greatest gift—is presence. When we love others, we open ourselves to their very being, we accept them as they truly are; they are present to us and we are present to them. In other words, when we love, we recognize and embrace the *heart* of another: his or her unique "presence" or personhood. We do not understand this presence—it is a *mystery* to us—and yet, we recognize that it exists, we accept it, we marvel at it and rejoice in it. This is also true in our relationship with God. For it is Presence that is the greatest gift—and the greatest grace—that even God can give us.[15] Without it, what would be the use of "religion"? What would be the use of heaven?

We often think of God's presence as an act of God, as something he *does*. We imagine that God "turns his eyes"—his attention—on us and makes himself present to us, perhaps because we are especially "holy" or "wise," or because he wants to send us on some special mission, as he did when he appeared to Moses. In other words, we think that, unless we somehow deserve God's gift of presence, he does not remember us, he is not there for us. But that is an absurd notion. Presence is not an "act" of God, it is the very *nature* of God. It is not what God *does*, but what God *is*.

God is One and Indivisible Infinity of Presence. When we begin to grasp this truth, we also begin to realize that God cannot *not* be present—be absent from us or forget us—just as he cannot be unmerciful or unjust. It is we who so often forget God; who are unwilling or unable to be present to him; who make ourselves absent from him. God is as present to us then as he is in our moments of deep prayer and love. We can perhaps even say that Presence is the Name of God, as far as it can be expressed in human speech; that God's mysterious words to Moses, "I am who I am," may be taken to mean "I am Presence: I am he who cannot ever be away."

It is only because God *is* Infinity of Presence, because he is the fullness of being, that he cannot be limited by anything finite: time, change, ignorance of any sort, forgetfulness or, above all, by any failure of love. It is only because he is Presence that we can say not only that he loves, but that God *is* Love. And that means God *cannot* cease to be present to us and love us; he is always, every second of earthly time as well as in eternity, totally present to us and totally *aware* of us.

Gaze of Love

We may find this truth surprisingly difficult to accept. Even in human relationships, we are most often afraid of too much presence, too much awareness. We may dislike it when others look at us too intently or for too long. We call it "staring" and feel that our privacy is being violated, our boundaries disregarded; we feel vulnerable and instinctively we retreat. Only in moments of deep passion or great love may we be willing to give another person the right to come so close to us: to gaze at us so fully.

How much more likely it is, then, that we may fear to open ourselves to the infinite awareness of God; that we may panic at the thought that God's gaze never wavers from us and shrink back from it in fear. This fear is not always the "holy fear" that Moses felt when God spoke to him in the desert; it may be an expression of the fear of *judgment* that many of us carry in our hearts. We may be projecting on God our own human tendency to judge, blame and criticize each other; to look at each other with disapproval and dislike, even hate.

When we think of God's unwavering awareness of us, we may think of the all-seeing "eye" of God glaring at us from above. "God sees everything you do and think," we may have been told again and again as children, "and, if you do wrong, he will punish you, even if nobody else does!" This is a tragic misunderstanding. God's awareness is not a matter of judging and punishing but of acceptance and love: it is the *gaze of love*. It is the life-giving rain that God sends on the wicked as well as on the just. It is an invitation to a relationship of true knowledge and trust.

We could not come into being or exist even for a moment without God's awareness resting upon us. It is this all-knowing, ever-present divine attention about which the Psalmist sang so gloriously:

> O Lord, you have probed me and you
>   know me; you know when I sit and
>   when I stand,
> you understand my thoughts from afar . . .
> Where can I go from your spirit? From your
>   presence where can I flee? . . .
> Truly you have formed my inmost being;
>   you knit me in my mother's womb.
> I give you thanks that I am so fearfully,
>   wonderfully made. (Psalm 139)

God's awareness is infinite, it is "fearful" to our minds and wonderful to our hearts: it is our very life.

For this life to become truly real for us, in order for us to be fully at peace before the gaze of God, fully open to his awareness of us, we must learn to respond to it in kind. We must be willing to open our awareness to God's awareness and to surrender ourselves to his love. Our love for God, like our love for each other, is not a matter of feelings or pious devotions but, first of all, a matter of presence: of willingness to forget ourselves and to focus all our attention on God.

Awareness of God

When we talk about our awareness of God we are not talking about some "higher," more spiritual way of prayer or meditation practice, but a very simple, ordinary human activity. We are talking about learning what is most natural to us, what our bodies and minds always do, but what we are most often too busy, too distracted, to be conscious of doing. We are talking about becoming more *attentive* to God in everything that *is*. We could also say that awareness of God is a way of *listening* to what God tells us in our everyday lives.

Awareness is much more like listening than like thinking or learning. When we are really listening to the voice of someone we love, or to great music, or to sounds of the natural world, we do not filter what we hear through thinking. We simply become *attentive* to it: we listen to it with our whole being, with our heart. In the same way, we try to be attentive, to listen, to everything in creation, for it all talks to us about God.

Above all else, we try to listen to ourselves, to our own hearts, for as St. Augustine has said, "We cannot find God, unless we find him in our own hearts."[16] Because we have been created in the image of God, we can see him and recognize him, however faintly, in the depths of our own being. This is why, when we learn to be more truly attentive to ourselves, when we try to listen more intently to what is really in our hearts, we always become more aware of God present in us and in every aspect of our life on earth.

The great paradox of awareness is that constant, simple attention to reality—to what is—*always* brings us into the presence of the Mystery at its heart. Whether we are attentive to the sky filled with stars or the tiniest insect crawling over a blade of grass, whether we are listening to a great spiritual teacher or a child's story, if our hearts are truly open, truly attentive, we will always find ourselves in the presence of God.

True awareness—true attention—opens the eyes of our heart to the immensity of our unknowing before the Mystery of God, but it also opens us to the *vision of faith* that has been given to us. For faith, although it cannot be achieved by any effort of the mind, is a gift—a *vision*—bestowed on the heart by God.

Part II

The Vision of Faith

The Vision of Faith

When we say that faith is a "vision," we do not mean that the source of our faith is some miraculous event or that we need to be convinced of its truth by apparitions, inner voices or other supernatural phenomena. These, it is true, may occur, for God can manifest his presence in many ways, but they are not necessary for the life of faith. They may in fact be detrimental to faith if we search for them and depend on them, or especially if we seek them for the emotional excitement—the thrill—they may give us. We must guard against the illusion that such events can ever be *proofs* of the truth of faith. As Christ said, those who do not believe will not believe even if "someone comes back to them from the dead." (Luke 16:30)

What, then, do we mean by the "vision" of faith? The word itself suggests a *seeing*: a manifestation of the Invisible Reality in a way that can be "seen" or apprehended only with the eyes of our heart. The vision of faith is an inner "epiphany": a shining forth of the Divine Light in the depths of our souls. It moves our hearts, and fills us with joy, and yet we cannot really define it or explain it to anyone. We cannot even explain it to ourselves. It is a mystery within the Mystery of God's love, and like love, it can only be experienced and embraced.

When we love, we know that the person we love is real, that our love is real. In the same way, we know that our faith is real, because when God makes his presence known to us, our hearts are filled with love. We are like the disciples whose hearts "burned within them" when Jesus walked with them on the road to Emmaus, even before they recognized him "in the breaking of the bread."

The "burning of the heart" does not necessarily mean a physical sensation in our physical heart, although we may at times experience it as such. It is above all a spiritual experience: an inner movement of love. Faith is our finite, human love responding to the Infinite Love of God. It is our true heart *recognizing* who stands at the door. It is "falling in love" with God. God's presence is love, it is the fire of the Spirit, and when we are touched by it, we *know* that it is real. We can never really forget it or deny it. Once we have seen it, we can never "un-see" it.

It is this tremendous vision of God who is Love, who is always present to us, always aware of us, who never forgets us or ceases to love us, who always reveals himself to those who long for him, that is the source of all our confidence and all our trust. This vision is the foundation of our faith.

Faithfulness and Love

We do not often think of faith in terms of "vision," presence, awareness or love. For most of us brought up in the Christian West, "faith" means, first of all, *acceptance* of a body of doctrine and morality that the Church has defined for us and to which we must assent. Secondly, "faith"—"the Faith"—is also taken to mean the whole *content* of this body of doctrine: the sum of all the teaching and life of the Church. Thus, we tend to think of faith in largely *impersonal* terms: we receive *it*, we accept *it*, we believe in *it*, we practise *it*.

The original biblical meaning of faith was quite different. In the Hebrew Bible, as in the New Testament, "faith" was something that could only happen between *persons*: it was only possible between those who loved and knew each other intimately and therefore trusted each other. Faith meant primarily a *relationship* of confidence and trust. To be "faithful" meant to be trustworthy: to keep all the promises and vows given to another. To "have faith" in others meant to believe that they would always *keep faith* with us—be "there," be present for us—whatever the cost.

To have faith, above all, meant to have faith in

God. Not in the *existence of God*, because that was never questioned—the world without God was inconceivable—but faith *in* God. Not in a distant and indifferent deity, but in God who was a Person, who revealed himself to his people, who loved them and was always present to them and aware of their needs; in God who was always *faithful* to them, whose words and promises were expressions of his infinite Being and were therefore infinitely trustworthy. No circumstances could change or limit them. God's promises *would* be fulfilled.

It was this kind of faith that God asked of Abraham and Moses, the prophets and the whole people of Israel. God called his people to believe that, however difficult and dark life became, whatever sorrows and disasters they had to face, he was never absent from them. The "faith of Israel" was the faith of a people that remained faithful to the Law—the commandments and the way of life and worship enjoined upon them—because in it they recognized the presence and voice of God, whom they loved and in whom they placed all their hope.

When we think of the long history of the Hebrew people, of the unspeakable suffering they have faced, it seems incredible that they could have persevered in their faith in God. And yet they did. It was not only great rabbis and saints who remained faithful, but countless ordinary Jewish men and women who, in the darkest of times, at the door of extinction, lit

Shabbat candles and sang of their love and trust in God. Even when they despaired and were angry at God, they still believed in him and longed for him. They died, as they lived, in the presence of God. This is a great mystery—the mystery of faith and love stronger than death.

Faith in Christ

This is also the kind of faith that Christ commanded his disciples to have in him and to preach to the world. To believe in Christ originally meant trusting him—in life as in death—and believing in his words and in his love. It meant recognizing that in him God was present and acting to fulfill his promises. All the "signs" or miracles Christ performed were manifestations of the Divine Presence—only God can heal, only God can forgive sins and grant eternal life.

For the disciples and all Christians since then, the most decisive sign of this Presence has been the Lord's resurrection from the dead. "Christ is risen!" is the fundamental Christian belief on which all other beliefs hinge. If Christ had not risen, our faith would have been in vain. (1 Corinthians 15:14) There would be no Christianity, because there would be no Christ among us. But if Christ, as Christians proclaim, is indeed alive—although in a manner we do not understand and cannot prove—then he is forever present with us. We can meet him and get to know him; we can recognize God in him; thus we can love, trust and believe in him.

When we say that we believe in Christ, we do not

mean we believe he was a great holy man, a teacher and a prophet, although he was all of those things. We believe in him because in him we recognize the Son of God—not as a figure of speech, but as reality. In other words, we believe in the Mystery of the Incarnation. This Mystery, like the Mystery of God himself, cannot be explained. It can only be pointed to, rejoiced in and revered. It can open our eyes to a dimension of reality, to the glory of the human person, that we never even knew existed.

To recognize God in Christ, we must first meet him in our own life. But how can we do this? We cannot experience his physical presence as the disciples could; we cannot hear his words, look into his face, see or touch him in some way. It is very unlikely that we shall meet Christ walking along some city street or country road, looking as we imagine him to have looked in the flesh, or as some religious artists have portrayed him. We are not likely to encounter him in someone at a local store who introduces himself as Christ. If someone does, we can be sure it is not he. How *can* we meet him, then? And when we do meet him, how can we be sure that we shall recognize God in him?

To this question there is no answer. It is like asking where and how we can first meet the person with whom we shall fall in love. We cannot arrange it, it just happens. We may meet somebody, listen to a talk, go to church with a friend, hear a story of great holiness or love. We may be pierced by a memory from childhood, an old prayer, our grandmother's icon, the ringing of bells, a song. Suddenly, we are filled with awe, our hearts are open and we recognize the Lord.

One Truth

Not everyone finds it possible to recognize God in the Person of Christ. Many have sought and found God in other religious traditions; many love and follow him on other paths. Christians are sometimes troubled by this fact, because they do not know how to reconcile it with their own faith in Christ. For if we believe that Christ *is* the Truth—the fullness of God's self-revelation—do we not also have to believe that *only* Christ can lead us to God? How can we maintain that there is only one way to Truth when we live in a world in which God is experienced and loved by countless wise and holy men and women of every religion and creed?

We do not know why God reveals himself in so many different ways. We may never be able to understand fully what Christ meant when he said that nobody can come to the Father except through him. (John 14:6) Perhaps "Christ" is the name for every true encounter with God; perhaps the Mystery of his Person is too big to be encompassed and expressed in any single way, and it is Christ who stands at every door that leads to Truth. As St. Ambrose is reported to have said in the fourth century, "All that is true, no matter who said it, is from the Holy Spirit."[17] This is another aspect of the Mystery of God, and we may be wise to accept it as such.

We may believe and we *must* hope that, at the End, when we finally see God face to face, we shall find that we have never been too far apart from all those who, in every age and in every tradition, have sought the Truth: that in the Presence of God, we have always been one. Such hope is not an expression of doubt and disbelief in the truth of our own path, but a sign of our realization of how infinite the Mystery of God is, and of how little we really know about God's final design for the world.

Still, it is important for us to remain faithful to the path on which God has placed us. And that means to remain faithful to him in whom we have recognized the Truth of God. We can be sure that for us, there *is* no truer way. We do not need to hide our conviction that the Christian Tradition contains the Good News of God's unconditional love that is essential for every human being to know. We do not need to apologize for our belief that Christ was the perfect expression of this love; that his life and his victory over death are, or can be, the source of great joy and hope for us all.

Christians, therefore, need not agonize over the fact that others may follow different paths. Rather, we should entrust each other to the mercy of God, learn from each other what we can, and rejoice that

God has never allowed us to forget him, that he has been found and loved in every manner, in every age and place. In the final analysis, the *heart of religion* is always, without exception, *love*. But we also need to learn to rejoice in our faith in Christ and to embrace him when we have found him. And, like the disciples, we must find out more about him; we must run after him and see "where he lives." (John 1:38)

Holy Tradition

The first "place" where most of us brought up as Christians will look for Christ is in what the Orthodox Church calls *the Holy Tradition*: the Scriptures (especially the Gospels), the Creed, the Liturgy, and the Sacraments (especially the Eucharist). We meet Christ and learn to know him in the whole, vast life and experience of the Church that has been handed down to us from the beginning and that shall continue until the "consummation" of all things at the End.

This is especially important for Western Christians to realize, for we most often think of the Tradition in terms of the authority of the Church (however we understand it) interpreting the teaching of Christ and the Apostles as recorded in the New Testament, and passing it down through the generations. The Tradition preserves, authenticates and interprets the Scriptures for us. Tradition, therefore, is understood primarily in terms of teaching, definition and interpretation.

But the Tradition is more than this. The Tradition, above all else, is *life*. It is the *Communion of Saints*: the living *presence* in our midst of Christ, the Apostles, the Fathers, and every Christian who has ever lived, believed and prayed. They are all with us; they are present and aware of us, as we are present and aware of them; they teach us, encourage us, cheer us on. Holy Tradition is the great, immense "place" of *presence*: the Mystery we are all invited to enter and share.

The Scriptures, the sacraments, the teachings, even the icons—the sacred art of the Eastern Church—are not merely ways of remembering Christ, as we remember some famous person from the past. They are rather, as both Catholics and Orthodox insist, means of making him *present* to us—of entering and sharing in the Divine Life he bestows. They are windows to the Invisible, doors to the Divine Presence. It is for this reason that the early Christians referred to them as "mysteries," and Orthodox Christians still do.

These mysteries must not be viewed as some kind of "holy magic." They do not snatch Christ out of heaven or make him materialize before our eyes. The mysteries are not ours to command or to manipulate, nor can they force or manipulate us. They do not make us holy automatically; they must be received by each of us into our own hearts.

The Holy Tradition is one immense river of the Living Water that Christ gives to us so that it may become *in us* "a spring welling up to eternal life." (John 4:14) We all live on the river's shore; we can point it out to each other and help each other to reach it, but we cannot force anyone to drink from it. We can only drink it and experience for ourselves its holiness and power. The Holy Tradition works only in the depth of our own hearts. It opens to us the immense treasure of the Divine Presence already among us and in us and *invites* us to enter it; it does not force us to come in.

The Creed

The same may be said of the solemn proclamation of the Christian Tradition: the Creed. We often think of the Creed as an official doctrinal statement of what we must believe. We call the teachings contained in the Creed "dogmas of the Church," and think of them as definitions of our faith. We give them our mental assent, but they do not always evoke in us any deeper experience of the Mystery of God; they do not make our hearts burn with love.

The word "dogma" seems a very beggarly way to refer to the great mysteries of our faith. It suggests "dogmatism," an attitude of the mind that considers its own understanding of the Tradition to be the only legitimate one and does not tolerate any other views. It encourages the illusion that we can contain the Mystery and enclose it in a formula that forever defines its nature, that we already possess the fullness of Truth.

We can *never* possess the fullness of Truth. There can be no final word about God. We cannot comprehend him finally, totally, even in eternity. We can only learn more and more about him and become more and more aware of him. We can only open ourselves to him ever more fully and never cease to rejoice in his presence. This infinite—never ceasing—learning is not only what heaven is really about, it is also what our life of faith on earth is about: more and more knowledge and awareness of God through ever greater love.

The Creed does not, therefore, "contain" God—does not place any limits within which we may experience him. The Mystery of God is bigger than the formulas that try to express God in words. As the *Catechism of the Catholic Church* states, "we do not believe in formulas but in the realities they express."[18] The Creed is an inspired image—a *true icon*—of the inexhaustible Reality of God and of his dealings with the world.

It is for this reason, perhaps, that the Eastern Church, following the ancient usage of the Fathers, rarely calls the truths contained in the Creed "dogmas" but refers to them as "mysteries."[19] They are not to be explained or too quickly defined, but proclaimed, reflected upon and approached with wonder and awe. The Creed is not a list of "facts" *about* God but an act of adoration of the mystery of God's love: a celebration of all he has done for us.

The Creed, like the sacraments, the icons, the prayers—our whole Tradition of Faith—cannot be grasped with our rational mind. The mysteries that it proclaims cannot be discussed or argued about (although there will always be theologians who will do so); they can only be received at the heart of our being, rejoiced in and embraced. If the words of the Creed do not become an expression of the Truth that we assent to and that our hearts also recognize and love, we may be unable to hold on to our faith and withstand for long the *doubt and disbelief* that so often attack us.

The Bearing of Doubt

It is *the bearing of doubt*, I think, that is our greatest fear and the heaviest cross on the way of faith. We doubt the vision, we doubt ourselves and we doubt God. Western Christians are especially prone to fear doubt and be tormented by it because of our tendency to expect that faith should give us an absolute, unshakeable *certainty* of what we profess to believe. When we doubt, we appear to question the truth of our religious beliefs. Doubt, therefore, is largely viewed as an *enemy of faith*. Doubt is seen as at best a trial, a temptation; at worst, a serious sin.

Not all doubt is dangerous to faith, however. Doubt can also be a necessary and *natural* reaction of human reason to any situation about which it does not have the final word. It appears to be our reason's job — the task assigned to it by God — to question every hypothesis and every conclusion it has reached, to re-examine its every assumption and never be afraid of being proven wrong.

Without this ability of human reason to *doubt itself*, to question and rethink its own solutions and conclusions, no progress in any field of knowledge and science would be possible. Doubt is a sign that the knowledge we possess can never be absolute, but must always remain *incomplete*. It can never exhaust all the infinite possibilities of reality, not even those that fall within the scope of rational thought; we can never entertain the illusion that we know it all. Doubt is the great enemy of "double ignorance"—the Socratic "gadfly" that will never let our minds go to sleep or be satisfied with any human wisdom, no matter how profound and interesting.

Without doubt, there could be no freedom of the mind. If we were never able to see alternative solutions to our problems, or different answers to our questions, there could be no possibility of error, but also no possibility of *choice*; there would be no doubt, but also no life of the mind. We would all be brain-dead.

Yet, like all other aspects of our nature, our reason—our thinking mind—may want too much. It may refuse to accept its own limitations; it may raise questions and demand rational answers in areas where there can be none. It may rebel against the "irrationality" of our religious beliefs and urge us to seek more "reasonable" solutions to the mystery of existence. We need to recognize this tendency of our reason, discern when it oversteps its boundaries, and learn to reject it.

Paradoxes of Faith

One of the most common sources of religious doubt is the necessity of expressing the mysteries of our faith in statements that seem paradoxical, even contradictory, and thus impossible for our thinking minds to reconcile. We are asked to believe in a God who is One and also Three; who is all good, and yet allows evil to exist in the world. We profess Christ who is truly man and also truly God, who died and yet is alive and present to us. We believe that we have been created free but also totally dependent on the omnipotent God; that we are mortal and yet survive death; that our bodies disintegrate—return to dust—and yet will "rise again." How can our reason cope with such paradoxical beliefs? How can we believe in them and remain rational?

These are not the grumblings of a rebellious mind, but questions that present themselves to any thinking person: to the believer as well as the unbeliever, to the religious person and skeptic alike. The source of most of the controversies or "heresies" that have caused so much dissension in the early Church lay precisely in the desire of some Christian theologians to get rid of the paradoxical nature of the truths of faith and choose only one side of each paradox.

Arians, for example, claimed that because God could not be subject to change, it would have been impossible for him to become man and that Christ, who was fully man, could not have been fully God. Nestorians insisted that God could not be born of a woman, and therefore Mary could not be the "Mother of God" and Christ's humanity could not have been totally real.

Pelagians insisted that human beings remained fundamentally free, and thus could work out their own salvation, while others believed that, because of the omnipotence of God, our eternal destiny depended only on the *choice* of God, and so we were all "predestined" either to be saved or to be damned. The Manicheans thought that because God could not be believed to be responsible for the existence of evil in the world, there had to be two gods: one responsible for the good, another for evil.

These heresies and many others like them reappear again and again in the history of Christianity, although in different guises and under different names. The main Christian Tradition, however, has always emphasized the need to hold onto *both* sides of each paradox. It has also insisted that the mysteries of faith must appear to us as paradoxes, because our minds cannot embrace the totality of the Mystery to which they point. They do not present different, contradictory truths, but are only *partial glimpses* of the One Unknowable and Inexpressible Truth.

We need to learn that the Divine Truth that our faith reveals to us can never completely satisfy or convince our rational minds. It will always remain a Mystery; our life of faith will always be a journey into the unknown, incomprehensible and often frightening reality of God. We must accept this fact of our life of faith and learn the *art of unknowing*.

Don't Know!

I once met a Korean Zen master who, after I had asked him some question I no longer remember, wagged his finger at me and said: "Thinking, thinking, thinking! Checking, checking, checking! No good! No good! *Don't know! Don't know! Don't know!*—That is your answer!" I don't think I really understood then what the master meant, but I never forgot him or his "answer." There was a joy in that meeting, a lightness of heart that I needed to touch when I felt confused, assailed by doubts, or in danger of taking myself too seriously.

It was only years later, after I had encountered the Eastern Christian Tradition and became more familiar with its teaching and, through it, with the teaching of the early Fathers, that I was able to understand his words better, and to recognize how relevant they were for the Christian way to God.[20]

I realized that we should never attempt to solve our doubts in matters of faith by rational arguments or inner debates. Such debates will only confirm our reason's illusion that Truth is subject to its judgment. If we refuse to accept our unknowing and search for some kind of "higher" or even esoteric knowledge that would explain it all, and forever do away with our doubts, our thinking may become ever more complicated and confused. We may get lost in a morass of speculation and mind-boggling interpretations, theories and fantasies. We may "solve" the Mystery but lose both our rationality and our faith.

Neither should we try to suppress our doubts, to push them away into some dark corner where they will fester and torment us even more. We must face our doubts, acknowledge them and simply let go of them. We shout "Don't know!" at them not as a sign of our confusion and disbelief, but as a sign of our assurance that Truth is immeasurably bigger than all our thinking and checking, and cannot be judged by anything we may think or not think about its nature. Doubt, like all products of thought, is irrelevant to faith.

If we keep doing that, if we *practice* "not-knowing," doubt—however distressing it may be—may yet prove to be not an enemy of our faith, but its ally and friend. Struggle with doubt may help us to understand ever more clearly the limits of thought, and thus become a training ground of faith: a powerful means of the "unknowing" that is the heart of faith.

There is no greater danger to faith, to wisdom and to love than the presumption that we know it all: that we have understood it all, that there is nothing more to discover or learn. Doubt makes it very difficult for us to fall into such a presumption.

It forces us to recognize how little we really know, how little we have understood, how much infinitely more there is to learn. Doubt makes it possible for us to approach the Mystery as if it were for the first time: with our hearts and minds open, ready to receive a new vision, ready to embrace it all over again. Doubt is the way of *beginning again.*[21]

Dangerous Doubt

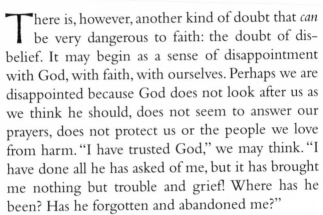

There is, however, another kind of doubt that *can* be very dangerous to faith: the doubt of disbelief. It may begin as a sense of disappointment with God, with faith, with ourselves. Perhaps we are disappointed because God does not look after us as we think he should, does not seem to answer our prayers, does not protect us or the people we love from harm. "I have trusted God," we may think. "I have done all he has asked of me, but it has brought me nothing but trouble and grief! Where has he been? Has he forgotten and abandoned me?"

Even more difficult for many of us to bear is the existence of so much evil and suffering in the world. Every day we hear about the murder, genocide or abuse of innocent people, including children. We hear about people dying of incurable and painful diseases, about natural disasters, about entire countries that lack food and clean water. How can we reconcile ourselves to all this suffering? How can we understand why God does not prevent it? Must we, like the Manicheans — ancient or modern — also believe that God can be both evil and good?

This painful and debilitating kind of doubt, the doubt of Job, may fill us with deep anxiety and discouragement. We may begin to question the truth of God's love and our own faith; we may begin to doubt the possibility of salvation — our own or the world's. We may feel that God is absent from us, or even convince ourselves that he does not exist.

We must fear this kind of doubt and struggle against it with all our strength, for it is dangerous — not only to the very foundations of our faith, but to our sanity as well. If we let it become rooted in our minds, it will grow and feed on our every weakness, on every sin we have ever committed or that has been committed against us. It will attack us every time we turn on the news or pick up a newspaper. It will change our world into absurdity, a universe from which God seems forever absent; and that is the true meaning of hell. In the end, it may lead us into despair and spiritual death. It is essential, therefore, for us to learn to discern such doubt in ourselves as soon as it arises, and fight it with every spiritual weapon at our disposal.

There can be no human answer to the problem of evil. Nothing we say or think will justify its existence. We can only cling to our faith and refuse to give in to despair. We can only trust that God, whose mercy and love are infinite, will one day let us see the sense of it all — that he will indeed wipe away every tear and change all suffering into joy. We can only fix our eyes on Christ, and remind ourselves that his victory over evil and death is to be ours as well. This, I think, is the only way to fight the doubt of disbelief. And we may have to fight it for as long as we live.

The Soil of Faith

While we are still on earth, we cannot prevent the doubt of disbelief from attacking us. We can never banish it forever from our minds and our lives. We cannot know *beyond any doubt* that God exists and that he is good. For, when we ask for faith without any doubt, we are asking for the kind of certainty or knowledge that is not possible for our finite minds to achieve. We are asking for a proof so extraordinary, so dramatic and powerful, that our minds would be overwhelmed by it and *forced* to believe.

In other words, when we ask for freedom from doubt, we ask God to take away our freedom to disbelieve—to say "no" to faith—and that is something God will never do. We shall be refused like the Pharisees were refused when they asked Christ for a "sign" that no one could refute.

And even if Christ were to grant some great sign to us, even if he appeared to us as he appeared to Thomas and showed us his wounds, would it really do us much good? Would we not soon get over our euphoria, our sense of certainty, and start doubting again? Asking for signs so that we can believe is like trying to fill a leaky bucket: it cannot be done.

Yet doubt is much more than a cross that we are forced to bear. Doubt—not just the "good" doubt of not knowing, but the pernicious doubt of disbelief as well—may become *rich soil* in which our faith can grow. Without ever experiencing doubt, we could become so satisfied with our weak faith, our puny love, our simplistic and sentimental piety, that we might never begin to seek the only proper "object" of faith, that is God.

Without doubt, we might never begin to look for God's presence and love. We might never learn to trust him. We might never encounter God in the reality of our own lives. For it seems that we do not usually begin to stretch the boundaries of our soul and search for a way to a bigger, more authentic spiritual life until we are pushed to it by our failure to understand, by our fear of unknowing and the pain of disbelief.

The Place of Safety

How, then, do we make sure that the "soil" does not become barren and the weeds of disbelief do not choke our little faith? How do we overcome doubt? We may have heard stories of dramatic battles that many saints have had to fight with doubt, some even to their last moment on earth. We may have heard of their discipline, ascetic labours and heroic prayer. Not all of us, however, are called to such greatness. Our common sense tells us that we do not have the courage, the stamina or the strength for it. We must find another, more humble way.

For most of us, the best way of overcoming doubt and disbelief may lie in flight. We may be wise to follow the example of St. Therese of Lisieux, who was tempted by agonizing doubt until the very end of her short life. When the temptation became too great, she told her sisters, she did not argue with it, she stopped struggling and just ran away![22] That is perhaps what most of us should do: look at the temptation to disbelief, recognize it for what it is, and flee.

There are many places that we can run to, many distractions and ways of avoiding or suppressing our doubts: we may have tried them all. But, as St. Therese well knew, there is only one place to which it makes sense for us to run, and that is into the arms of God. When we are in the arms of God—in *God's presence*—we are truly safe from every temptation or doubt. Only there is it possible to have unshakeable faith. Only in the presence of God is it possible to move beyond paradoxes and clever arguments, beyond every doubt and fear, and simply rest in the Mystery.

When we find ourselves in that Presence, it may be that our greatest surprise, and our greatest joy, will lie not in the discovery of any "answers" to the questions that may have tormented us, but in the discovery of how powerless these questions are, how incapable they are of destroying the vision of faith that had been—once and for all—bestowed on us. For God never withdraws his gifts.

In the presence of God, we realize that our doubts, even our disbelief, are like clouds that have confused us and obscured the clear sky of God's goodness and love for a moment. We realize that our doubts have not made any impact on the Truth of God, not even a scratch; that the inexpressible and unknowable mysteries of our faith—of God, of Christ, of all the teachings of our Tradition—are still there, as certain and as indestructible as they have always been. We rejoice in God, whose greatness is incomparable to anything we could ever understand or imagine and whose beauty is beyond description. We are overwhelmed by the beauty of our God and of the path on which he has placed us.

A Hymn of Beauty

Joseph Raya, the former Byzantine Rite Arch-bishop of Galilee, never tires of reminding us of this most important "fact" about God. At every Liturgy, in every homily and at every dinner table he repeats this obvious and yet oft-forgotten truth. "My children," he says, "how very beautiful is our God! How beautiful is our religion! Never, *never* forget that!"

Every time I hear him say this I realize, once again, that this *is* the Good News, the heart of our vision of faith, the most important thing we need to know about God and about Christianity: *God is so beautiful*. We search for him and long for him not because we want to be good or wise, not even because we are afraid that if we do not find him we shall go to hell, but only because God is so beautiful that we cannot help longing for him! We believe in the truth of our religion not because we have been taught to believe in it, but because it is so glorious, so overflowing with beauty, that our hearts cannot help wanting to embrace it, to become immersed in it, and to remain forever in its glory.

Recently, I came across the words of the Council of Chalcedon proclaiming, in AD 453, the Mystery of the Incarnation of God in Christ. As I was reading them, I thought about how powerfully they reflect this glorious nature of the Christian Faith.

> We teach that the one and only Son of God, our Lord Jesus Christ, is the very same one perfect in divinity, and the very same one perfect in humanity. He is the very same God, consubstantial with the Father, according to his divinity, and the very same person, consubstantial with us, according to his humanity. He is the one and same Christ in two natures ... without change, without confusion, without division, without separation. . . .

This, I realized, is not a dry definition of doctrine, but a *prayer*, a hymn of such beauty and power that it pierces the heart and makes the intellect still and silent before the Mystery it proclaims. It is a poem, a shout of joy.

To understand faith as the joyous, natural and yet deeply spiritual human response to the beauty of the Divine Presence whenever we encounter it is, I believe, to discover the true joy of the life of faith. It is perhaps what Christ meant when he *commanded* us to have joy. He could not have done so unless he knew, in the way that may take us a lifetime to discover, that true joy is a gift available to all: that we can all search for it and find it. To quote Archbishop Joseph again, "Joy is not an option, it is an obligation for Christians."

Joy

In the language of Christianity, joy is not merely a human emotion but a spiritual experience. Joy comes to us from a place outside ourselves, or from a place so deep in our hearts that we cannot summon it by an act of will. It is a "fruit of the Holy Spirit" (Galatians 5:22), a *grace*. This is why we are always, as C. S. Lewis has said, "surprised by joy." It bursts upon us unawares, in moments of prayer and praise, but we can also experience it in some great human happiness, in a world filled with beauty, in moments of deep love.

We are not called to be joyful only in the contemplation of beauty, or in the peace and satisfaction of a happy life. We are called to joy even in the midst of suffering and death, of persecution, abuse and sin. For God is present even in the hell we make for each other; as the multitude of saints as well as very ordinary men and women have witnessed, our hearts can see him there and rejoice in his presence and love. It is to give us this power of joy—in the good and in the bad—that Christ won his victory on the Cross. This is the greatest proof of the truth of our faith that we could ever ask for or imagine: that even hell cannot destroy our joy in what we believe.

But Christ also showed us the price we must pay for this immense gift. For there is only one way to such joy: we can find it only by turning away from ourselves—by forgetting ourselves—and giving all our attention and all our trust to God. Joy is a spontaneous response of the human spirit when it is able to step beyond the confines of its own ego and finds itself in the presence of God. In hell we know and recognize God in the same way we know and recognize him in heaven: only through love.

Because joy is an inner experience of the presence of God—a relationship—it is impossible to categorize it or define it in words. Like love itself, it cannot be taught. Each human being must find his or her own path to its door. For a few it may be a "high road" of contemplation, of ecstasy and bliss. To most of us, however, joy comes in small doses, in short, faint glimpses of the Mystery of God present in the midst of our ordinary lives.

Whatever way it comes, joy is always a sign that we are beginning to know God in the only way God can be known—through *love*; that our hearts are open to this love, that we are beginning to allow ourselves to be touched and transformed by it. For if our faith is to become real—a real expression of who we truly are—we must allow God to enter our own reality, our own hearts. To find God, we must allow him to reproduce, as it were, the Incarnation of his Son in our own being, in our own life, and to transform us into "another Christ," as St. Paul expressed it. This is what the early Christian Fathers and Mothers called "true conversion" (in Greek, metanoia)—a radical "change of heart" or mind.

Part III

Conversion of the Heart

True Conversion

We usually think of "conversion" in terms of embracing a new faith or way of life. Most often, we think of it as converting *others* to the Truth that we are convinced we already possess. And yet, as we have seen, we can never possess the fullness of Truth. We can only receive its light into our own hearts and allow it to radiate from there in its own time and in its own way.

We cannot really convert another person to anything, for we cannot undergo a change of heart for anybody else. We can only — with great difficulty and much pain — undergo it ourselves. We can only fall in love with God ourselves, for love must come as our own free gift. We should not presume, therefore, to judge the truth of other people's faith, or badger them to embrace what they are unable to love, but concentrate on our own conversion and strive to make our faith real — incarnated — in our own lives.

True conversion is not a question of changing our opinions or beliefs, but of changing our hearts: our fundamental way of experiencing ourselves and the world. It involves a complete *transformation* of our lives through letting go of our *egotism*, our self-preoccupation, and surrendering ourselves—all of ourselves—to God so that we may be filled with his love. Conversion is *a choice for love.*

Conversion is the price and the grace of discipleship; it is what Christ called us to do when he said that we should "lose" or "deny" ourselves, take up our "daily cross" and follow him (Luke 9:23-24). We encounter Christ and through him, God, only in a life of love: the love of God and the love of others. Christ himself made this absolutely clear. If we want to be his disciples, if we hope that he will acknowledge us as such, we must love one another. This is the first and the second commandment, the only one by which we shall be judged. God is love, and he can draw us into himself, but only if we love.

When we embrace the path of conversion, we try to let go of everything in ourselves that is false—*that is not love*—and thus takes us away from God. We pray that one day, perhaps only for a moment, we may become, as Catherine Doherty often said, "a light to our neighbour's feet"; that another may be able to glimpse, however dimly, Christ living in us; that something we say or do, perhaps a little gesture of love we make, may be for someone a reminder, a call, a glimmer of hope. That is really the only way we can convert anyone.

Metanoia is a difficult, never-ending task. There are moments of rest, of joy, when our hearts are truly emptied of our self-absorption and we are able to glimpse God and rejoice in him in our own hearts. For most of us, however, such moments soon pass and we must take up our work again. The Christian path is one of unending conversion: the *narrow path* of repentance and love.

The Narrow Path

Western Christians do not often understand the real meaning of repentance. Rather than seeing it as a way of conversion and trust in God's infinite mercy, we tend to view it as an expression of an exaggerated, even neurotic way of guilt and self-blame. Seen in this light, repentance focuses our attention only on our imperfections and sins — a very one-sided way of looking at ourselves. If we dwell so much on the dark side of our nature, we might object, how can we ever discover the goodness and love at the core of our being? How can we learn to see in ourselves an image of God? How can we see the image of God in others? How can repentance be a path of learning to love?

Christian repentance means much more than dwelling on our sins. It is true that we must regret and ask forgiveness for many things in ourselves and in our lives; to deny this fact would be a sign of spiritual blindness. We have all sinned, we have all hurt each other, we have all failed to love. We need to learn to face that fact — not with anxiety and guilt, but with humility and trust.

We also need to remind ourselves of what we have already learned in our search for the truth of ourselves: that most often we can come to it only *negatively*, as it were, by "letting go of lies." This also applies to the perfection that we often think we should have but never seem to reach in this life. We can never be really good, for "only God is good." (Matthew 19:17) We are not able to grasp perfection in one big swoop. We do not walk our path to perfection — to holiness — by leaving all our burdens and failings at the starting point! We drop them one by one — we repent of them — as soon as we recognize them, and we leave them at the feet of God.

When we repent, we realize how weak and limited we are, how far from the perfection that we long for. Perhaps this realization makes us sad. But we also realize that the love and mercy of God are infinitely greater and more powerful than our sins; that, before the face of God, they are nothing at all. As Metropolitan Anthony Bloom once told me, "Our sins are nothing to God. One 'puff' of his breath, and they are all blown away!"

Our practice of repentance can teach us this essential truth, and an even greater one: when we repent, we do much more than bring our sins to God. We present *ourselves* — all that we are — to him and surrender to him all the burdens we bear: all our disappointments, our sorrows, our anxieties, our hurts. We surrender all that we have done to others, "intentionally or inadvertently," as the Eastern

Church prays, but also all that has been done to us and to the world. In other words, we surrender all of our human reality, what the Christian Tradition calls "the condition of man."

As we learn to open ourselves more and more to the love and mercy of God, we begin to see ourselves, as well as all other people, as if through the eyes of God. We see ourselves in the light of God's constant, faithful love and we can at last shed the burden of our hypocrisy and pretense and just be ourselves. We realize that we do not *need* to prove anything to God or to anybody else: that there isn't and never has been a standard we must meet or an exam we must pass. We learn to accept and be glad of our human reality.

Through the faithful, daily practice of repentance, we begin to realize that underneath the darkness of our weakness and sin lies a deeper truth. The path we have embraced has led us to a true understanding: not only of who we are in ourselves, but above all of who we are in the eyes of God. And to discover this truth is a very great joy!

The Prayer of the Heart

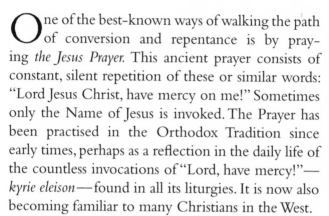

One of the best-known ways of walking the path of conversion and repentance is by praying *the Jesus Prayer.* This ancient prayer consists of constant, silent repetition of these or similar words: "Lord Jesus Christ, have mercy on me!" Sometimes only the Name of Jesus is invoked. The Prayer has been practised in the Orthodox Tradition since early times, perhaps as a reflection in the daily life of the countless invocations of "Lord, have mercy!"— *kyrie eleison*—found in all its liturgies. It is now also becoming familiar to many Christians in the West.

The Jesus Prayer is often called "the prayer of the heart." This is usually taken to mean that, as we are saying it, we should focus our inner attention on Christ who lives in us, and try to say the words not with our lips, but to let them come from our heart, the centre of our being. Many of the early teachers of the Prayer recommended this way of "centering" our attention while praying it and thus "entering the heart" in order to find God living there. They sometimes referred to it as "praying with our hearts." If we pray that way, they taught, we may eventually realize and experience, sometimes in very extraordinary and unexpected ways, God's presence within us.

The true power of the Jesus Prayer, however, does not lie in any extraordinary gifts that it may bestow on us. On the contrary, the practice of the Prayer can be incredibly powerful and effective for us because it is so simple and so *austere*: because it helps us to put aside our own words and ideas, our own habits of thinking and feeling, and connects us with a centuries-old tradition of prayer in which generations of Christians have found a way of being present and real before God.

We should never assume that the Jesus Prayer — or any other way of prayer — is the only way, or even the best way, of being present to God. If we are drawn to it and have the grace to persevere in it, it may be the best way for us, but not necessarily for others, who must search for God in other ways. The best way, the only way, each one of us should pray is the one that moves our own heart and opens it to God.

I once heard a story that illustrates this essential point well. Many years ago, a friend told me, she confessed to a wise old priest that, having practised the Jesus Prayer for many years, she still could not "pray it with her heart" as she had heard she should. "I repeat the words of the Prayer over and over again," she complained, "but I still do not know the way to my heart and how to find God living there!"

The old priest did not seem very sympathetic. "Stop paying attention to yourself," he told her, "and attend to him to whom you are trying to pray!"

"But, Father," she protested, "am I not supposed to find Christ in my heart and pray to him there?" "What difference does it make where you find him?" he asked. "You haven't got him locked up inside you, you know! He is inside you as well as outside; he is in front and behind, below and above. So pray to him always, wherever it is possible for you to find him, and you will soon find him in your heart as well!"

The words of the old priest can shed much light on the path of prayer. We *must* seek God where he is most present to us and in the way that it is most real for us. If we do that, we shall soon learn to find and recognize his presence everywhere. We shall learn the way of "ceaseless prayer" to which St. Paul called us. (1 Thessalonians 5:17) We shall be filled with joy and our hearts will burn within us: *that* is how we shall "find our hearts" and know we have found God. In the most fundamental sense, all true prayer is "prayer of the heart."

As my old friend Mother Macrina used to say,

> "There are not many 'kinds' of prayer, or ways of 'doing' it—only one. To pray is to be in God's presence, and nothing else can be called 'prayer' at all. . . . When you are in God's presence, you can 'do' or 'say' whatever you wish. You can ask for anything you need, repent for your sins, be silent or talk, sing, dance or even stand on your head!"[23]

Silence Before God

There are, of course, moments in our life with God when we really do not want or need to talk or do anything, when just being in his presence is enough. This is the silence of "falling out," we might say — not only beyond words or thoughts, but also beyond the world of *self*. It is the true silence of contemplation, the silence of Presence.

If we always try to pray as simply and as truthfully as we can, if in our prayer as in our whole spiritual life we seek only God, we shall probably experience moments of such silence — moments when we are truly able to still our frantic minds and are embraced by the great silence of God. It is this kind of prayer — the *prayer of silence* — that most writers on the subject agree is the crown of spiritual life.

There is, however, no technique that will lead us to this silence. We cannot learn it or make it happen. It is a grace, a gift of God. It is a glimpse of heaven on earth. Perhaps it is God's way of reassuring us that we are on course, and that he is very near. Or, we might say, it is like a visit home, a rest from all the strain and struggle of our everyday Christian life.

Yet we should not be worried or discouraged if we experience such moments only rarely, or never at all. We need to remind ourselves that achieving them is not the task we are asked to undertake. Our most important task in learning to pray—our *only* task—is to be present to God, just as we are. We may hope and pray for the grace to experience such moments—there is nothing wrong with that. We should receive them, when they come, with gratitude and joy, but we cannot expect them to become our everyday experience on this earth. We should try not to cling to them but to let them go.

There is a story of St. Catherine of Siena that I like very much. I am not sure if it is literally true, but I hope it is, because it seems so real; it seems to describe something that God would do. It is said that St. Catherine was so happy being alone with God, so filled with joy and love, so caught up into a silent ecstasy of Divine Love, that she had no desire ever to leave her cell.

One day, however, Christ appeared to her and told her to go back into the world and do some work for him. Catherine apparently objected and complained. "I do not want to go anywhere," she said, "I only wish to stay here with you." "Well, then," Christ told her, "You can stay here by yourself, if you wish, but *I* am going to do the work that must be done." Needless to say, Catherine went.

That, it seems to me, is the best definition of "true prayer" that we can have: doing whatever must be done—whatever God asks us to do—in his presence. It is being always totally present and *available* to God. This availability is what the Christian Tradition understands by *obedience* to the will of God.

Total Love

Too often we think of obedience to the will of God in terms of submission to an awesome and arbitrary Divine Power whom we fear and do not wish to offend, whom we *must* obey if we want to be accepted and approved. This is the kind of obedience we often confuse with the heroic obedience of the saints.

True obedience, however, is not a slavish abdication of our freedom and dignity as persons, nor an expression of emotional dependence, but a free and mature gift of total availability: *total love*. Christian obedience is inconceivable, a contradiction in terms, unless it is the obedience born not of fear but of love. It is this obedience that we pray for, as Christ told us to do, when we pray that the kingdom of God may come and his will may be done "on earth as it is in heaven."

It is also the kind of obedience that the author of the Letter to the Hebrews must have had in mind when he applied these words of the psalmist to Christ (10:7): *Here am I, Lord, I come to do your will.* (Psalm 40:7, 8) Christ came into the world to be totally present and available to God—"even unto death"—and thus to show us the true way of doing

God's will. What is asked of us is not sacrifices and oblations, but obedience of love and limitless *trust*. The saints understood this and lived it every day of their lives. Sanctity, I once heard someone say, is the ability *to extend our own will to embrace the whole mystery of the will of God*. This challenge is not for the fearful or the weak!

The saints try to be present and always available to God because they have already learned to believe that whatever God asks of them, however difficult and incomprehensible it may seem to them at times, is not an arbitrary demand or some kind of test, but an expression of his love. They have learned to believe that the will of God—all that he sends them—is or can become the means of transformation: their own and that of all those whose lives they touch.

We realize that we do not yet have such heroic faith and trust. We suspect that God's will might be too heavy a burden for us to carry. We still need to protect ourselves from the pain of the transformation that we fear might crush us. When faced with suffering and evil that seem too great to be borne, we are tormented by rebellion and doubt.

And yet, the vision of faith has already touched us; we have already begun to believe. We are therefore prepared to stake our lives on the conviction, however weak it may be, that God knows what each of us needs to reach the fullness of life for which he has created us. We strive, therefore, every day and every moment, to allow God's will to be completed in us. We strive to surrender ourselves to him in everything he asks of us, to accept everything he sends us. We try to be more present and available to God: more aware of him in the ordinary, everyday reality of the world that surrounds us, in the people we encounter and, above all, in the depths of our own hearts.

Remembering God

Such obedience — such availability — is not some-thing we can achieve on our own. True obedience is the fruit of love: our love for God and God's love for us. It is the fruit of a life of ceaseless prayer, of a life lived in the presence of God.

The seventeenth-century Carmelite Brother Lawrence gave witness to the possibility of such a life in his every letter and in every conversation of his that has been recorded. "Prayer was nothing else for him but a sense of the presence of God," one of his friends reported. "And, when the appointed times of prayer were past, he found no difference, because he still continued with God . . . so that he passed his life in continual joy." Nothing diverted him from prayer, we are told, because the smallest thing done in the presence of God — even "picking up a straw from the ground" — was for him true prayer and practice of the presence of God.[24]

The secret of true prayer, as of the whole Christian life, is to *remember* God in everything we do, in everything we say, in everything that happens to us. It is not remembering in the sense of recalling someone we knew in the past, or someone who is away from us, but in the sense of becoming aware again of someone who is always *here*, but to whom we have not been paying any attention, whose presence we have forgotten. *Becoming aware* of and attentive to God is our true response to God's presence and unceasing awareness of us.

But how is this to be done? How can we remember God in our active, noisy lives? How can we remember God always, or even a few times a day? And, if we do remember him, how can we prevent ourselves from forgetting again?

This may be especially difficult for us, living in a world almost totally deprived of the daily reminders of God that most people in most other centuries and cultures found at every turn. There are no bells ringing from our churches at regular intervals, no symbols of faith displayed anywhere, no prayer flags, no calls to prayer. It is not easy to remember God in a world that has almost totally forgotten him. This is why we must *work* at it. We must practise remembering God, just as we must practise everything else in our spiritual life.

The Practice of Remembering

We practice this first of all by simply reminding ourselves as often as we can of the *fact* of God's presence: that he is always here, always aware of us; that his gaze of love never wavers from us. We remind ourselves that we *already* live in his presence, whether we know it or not. Otherwise, we would have ceased to exist.

But because our daily lives are so often empty of God, we must give ourselves a chance to remember him more easily. We need, especially at the beginning, to clear a silent space—a bit of time—in our daily lives in which to try to focus our attention on God more intently. We may find that liturgical prayer—the daily offices and prayers of the Church—helps us to remember God. Or we may discover that a faithful practice of the Jesus Prayer or a similar short prayer, perhaps a verse from the Psalms, is the simplest, the most spiritually economical way to remind ourselves of God's presence. We may find it useful to connect our practice with some regular, daily activity: getting up, sitting down to meals, driving to work.

There is no one method for remembering God that all can follow, just as there is no one method of prayer that works for everybody. But if we realize how important it is to be in God's presence, how much we *long* for it, we shall find a way. We shall use our own ingenuity to find it for, as *The Cloud of Unknowing* tells us, "It is best to learn these methods from God by your own experience rather than from any man in this life."[25]

If we persevere in this work, if we hold on to our trust and always call on his help, then in God's good time, the grace of living in his presence will surely be given to us. We shall realize that we remember God more and more often; that we are aware of him for longer and longer periods of time. We shall discover that this has changed not only the way we pray, but also the way we view our religion, ourselves and the whole of our earthly reality. We shall at last feel truly at home with God, with the world and with ourselves.

Living the Life of Heaven

It has been said that becoming truly aware of God's presence is like discovering another dimension of reality that has always been there but that we have not noticed before.[26] Every moment of our lives, everything we do or experience is now seen as if in a great light that has been lit beyond the horizon of our everyday life. The eyes of our minds and hearts are opened to a new reality, a new way of experiencing ourselves and the world. Everything has become prayer for us.

A monk I know likes to say that Christianity is not a religion, but a way of *living the life of heaven* while still on earth. Heaven is Presence; it is the Glory of God unveiled; it is our small, finite life illumined and transformed by the light of eternity. Heaven — the "place" where we hope to go after death — is the *fulfillment*, not the beginning, of our eternal life. The beginning is made here on earth every time we open ourselves to the presence of God.

The saints often insist on the reality of this truth. *Every* little thing we do in the presence of and for the love of God, every word we say and every breath we take, is *sacramental* and transforms the world. As seen through the eyes of faith, there are no special vocations or great deeds. There is only the work we have been asked to undertake, the talents we have been given to develop, the people we have been asked to love, the world around us whose stewards we have been called to become. There is only our duty of the moment.

We do not often do this work well. We are not attentive, we get bored, we long for another, more interesting task. "Picking up straws" from the ground, day after day, so often seems to be a total waste of our energy and time. We daydream, we grumble and complain. "How can this be the life of heaven?" we ask. "This is purgatory, at best!" We forget, perhaps, that purgatory is the vestibule of heaven; we are fortunate indeed if we find our way into it while still on earth.

Mother Maria Gysi used to say that "we are all unprofitable servants."[27] How clearly we begin to see the truth of that statement in the light of God's presence! How clearly we begin to see all our failures, our shoddy work, our time spent grudgingly! But we also realize that we need not become discouraged or burdened with guilt. We need only remind ourselves that God never turns away from us, that the life of heaven is never closed to us. We do not live it by our "successes" at holiness but by unceasing conversion, repentance and love; we live it by *trying to live it* again and again. This is all we are asked to do.

I wish it were possible to express this idea even more clearly so that we could truly understand it. So much of our fear and disbelief, our sad and empty lives, is unnecessary, even absurd, because we have forgotten (or perhaps never learned) this immense, astounding truth: the kingdom of God is already among us and in us. We are already being transformed, filled with God's life, radiant with the light of his glory.

The Glory of Man

The goal of conversion or transformation through repentance and love is most often expressed in the Western Christian Tradition as growing into a *union with God*: a union so close, so intimate, that it can be viewed as becoming one with God. The Eastern Church goes even further than that. The Eastern Fathers talk of the way of transformation as *divinization* or deification of a human person: a process through which God, in a manner totally incomprehensible to human reason, transforms us so totally, so radically, that we can dare to say that we become "god." St. Athanasius wrote in the fourth century, "God became man so that we could become god."[28]

The Western Church, on the whole, has shied away from using the term "divinization" because it seemed too radical, too easy to misunderstand. It may seem to suggest the possibility of human beings transcending their human nature and becoming divine. "Union with God" appeared to be less ambiguous, a little easier to express in the language that the Western mind (or Western theologians) could accept.

Divinization, however, is never understood as a process by which a human being sheds his or her human nature and assumes the nature of God. Such a concept is as foreign and as unacceptable to the Christian East as it is to the West. The Christian way of transformation is never understood as a way of "self-transcendence," of the dissolution of our human self and "merging with God," as it is understood in some religious traditions. We do not merge with God; we enter into *communion* with him.

Because we have been created in the likeness and image of the Person of God, our personhood is not an extra frill added to our humanity, but our true reality, our true being. We can *never* be dissolved—cease being a person—in this life or in eternity. We are converted, we are transformed, but we always remain what we have been created to be—human persons, ourselves.

Whether we talk about divinization or about union with God, all Christians agree that transformation cannot be achieved by us alone, but only by God living and acting within our hearts. Through prayer and repentance, we can and must "empty ourselves" in order to create a *space* for God to work in, but it is he who transforms us by his sovereign grace, by sharing his divine life with us.[29] In other words, God makes us *holy*—makes us "whole"—by *completing* with his own life and spirit all that is lacking in us, all that is not yet fully formed, all that has not yet grown to the full stature required of the "children of God."

It is in this sense that we must understand St. Paul's teaching about our adoption by God. We are able to share in the glory that was Christ's by nature only because we have been "adopted" by God. (Romans 8:15) Our own human nature is not "transcended" or discarded but brought to fulfillment, brimming with life and glorified with Christ. There can be no vocation, no glory higher than that.

Christic Within

To be truly alive, truly "whole"—filled with the life and glory of God—is the meaning and the goal of our Christian life. We are transformed, we become another Christ, by becoming vessels of the Divine Presence. This is the Christian teaching of the *indwelling* of God in the human heart.

Indwelling is the mysterious gift promised by Christ as the fruit of love: God's love for us as well as our love for God and for each other. If we love God, and if we love each other, he will come and "abide" in us. (John 14:23) The mystery of the divine indwelling suggests an intimacy of the relationship—of communion—between God and us that no human mind could ever dare to imagine, but of which our faith assures us. It is the goal of our path but also the reality of our life of love.

It is possible to say that Christ's teaching on the divine indwelling sums up and expresses as fully as it can be expressed the purpose of the Incarnation. It signifies the fulfillment of all the promises God made to his people from the very beginning. It restores to us the state of being that was given to us at the moment of creation, and opens to us again the path of closer and closer communion with God that God has, from the beginning, intended us to walk. Christ came to make it possible for us to fulfill God's original plan.

When we become "another Christ" we do not only become like him, we become truly transformed into him. His spirit becomes our spirit; our heart is filled with his own divine energy and life. He becomes our own inner life, our heart of hearts, our "true self." He is *the Christ, the Lord within*. This is why we cannot really know God until we "enter our hearts" and unite ourselves with Christ — God-made-flesh — who lives in us.

It is there, in the innermost part of our being, that we truly see God: we live his life, we *know* him in a communion of love. But it is also only there — united with him — that we become truly aware of his presence *outside* of ourselves, at the heart of all reality. For God, as the old priest told my friend, there is no "inside" or "outside," no "below" or "above," no "before" or "after." In the presence of God all things, all dimensions, all levels of reality are transformed and glorified.

Why do we not reflect on this amazing truth more often? Why do we not rejoice and glory in it? Perhaps we are afraid of what it may cost us. Or perhaps we are so obsessed with being "good," with "deserving" heaven, that we have no time to reflect on the life of heaven open to us already *now*, on earth. And yet, this is why Christ knocks at the door of our innermost being: to unite himself with us, to become our daily bread, our own eternal life. Until we have understood this and have opened the door, we have not understood anything at all.

When we insist on the reality of our transformation, we are not insisting on glorifying ourselves or claiming divinity for even a part of ourselves. We are, rather, proclaiming a *mystery*: the Mystery of God, the mystery of his love, but also the mystery and the glory of the human person, the mystery of the finite overflowing with the Infinite, the visible aflame with the Invisible and lighting up the world.

Consuming Fire

The Christian Tradition sees the Hebrew image of the burning bush — of the ordinary burning with the flame of the Extraordinary — as repeated and fulfilled by the vision of Christ, the Light of the world unveiled, drawing the whole universe to himself and transforming it into himself. The clearest example, or icon, of this vision is found in the New Testament story of the *Transfiguration*.

We are told that one day, shortly before his death, Christ took his closest disciples — Peter, James and John — to a high mountain. There he was transfigured before them: "*his face shone like the sun and his clothes became white as light. And behold, Moses and Elijah appeared conversing with him . . . and a bright cloud cast a shadow over the disciples and from the cloud they heard a voice saying, 'This is my beloved Son, with whom I am well pleased; listen to him.'*" (Matthew 17:1-6)

The Light of the Divine Presence always shines at the heart of creation. While we cannot often recognize it, the saints can. For holiness is not perfection — the absence of any weakness or sin — but rather openness to God, willingness to let him transform us and thus become channels of God's holiness for the world. Saints are those who live before the face of God.

This is why they sometimes appear, like Moses, shining with a light so bright that we must avert our eyes and ask them to veil their faces. The image of this "uncreated light" in religious iconography is the halo surrounding the faces and bodies of saints.

The light shining in and around the saints is not a cool, gentle light. It is the blazing light of the consuming fire that Christ came to cast upon the earth. (Luke 12:49) It is the "living flame of love," as St. John of the Cross experienced it.[30] It burns and transforms all those whom it touches.

In the Stories of the Desert Fathers, it is said that Abba Lot went to see Abba Joseph to ask the holy man what he, Lot, must do to become a true monk. "You cannot be a true monk," Abba Joseph replied, "*unless you become like a consuming fire.*" He stood up and stretched out his hands and his fingers became like ten lamps of fire. "If you will, *you can become all flame,*" he said.[31]

Such manifestations of the divine fire are not totally unknown in recent times. St. Seraphim of Sarov, the great saint of pre-revolution Russia, seems to have had the gift of radiating the light of God. People who knew him often reported this fact, although he always asked them not to talk about it to others.[32] In a more ordinary way we, too, may have encountered men and women whose faces seemed to shine with an inner light and in whose presence we felt very close to God.

Even if we are not able to accept the literal truth of such experiences, they still provide us with a powerful image of the reality of the light and fire of God's presence in the world and in the human heart. The light of the saints represents the highest fulfillment of the Christian vocation and of Christian hope.

Theotokos

For most Christians, Eastern and Western, the most exalted embodiment of the reality of their hope is the person of Mary, the Mother of God. In both the Catholic and the Orthodox Traditions, she is an example and a sign of the glorious destiny that "the eye has not seen, the ear has not heard, that has not entered the human heart, but that God has prepared for those who love him." (1 Corinthians 2:9)

Christian imagination has always loved to dwell on the Virgin and Mother and to see in her, as in a perfect mirror, the glory of all creation. The saints never tire of extolling her beauty. "The light of God surrounding her as she bears her Son in her womb," the Church sings, "amazes the universe."[33] Devils flee at the sight of her and the angels bow down before her.

Archangel Gabriel, as he approaches her to announce the Good News of the Incarnation of God in her, "is rapt in amazement" as he beholds her splendour. "By what name shall I call you?" he cries out. "I am bewildered, I am lost! I shall greet you as I was commanded to do and say: Hail, O Woman, full of grace!"[34] She is the tent of the Divine Presence pitched at the centre of human reality. She is also the "*burning bush*," for the fire of the Divine Presence is within her. She is the perfect *icon of the Incarnation*. She is the *Theotokos*, the God-Bearer.

This is why the iconography of the early Church and of the Orthodox Church even now never, or hardly ever, represents her alone, but always with her Son, pointing him out to the world. Mary embraces and *encloses* the whole "event" of the Son of God in the flesh. She receives him in her womb and gives him birth. She protects him and looks after him until it is time to let him go out on his mission. And at the end, when "all is accomplished," when he has died and is taken down from the Cross, she receives him again into her arms.

And yet, as Mother Maria Gysi insisted, although her glory as the Mother of the Divine Son is hers alone, because she is "unambiguously" human, everything we say of her, every expression of reverence and love, can also be applied to each truly converted and transformed human person — "another Christ," a saint. Every Christian has been called to the same vocation: to open ourselves to the Spirit of God "and to allow him to reproduce in us the Incarnation of the Son of God. . . . So the exaltation of the Mother of God quite simply means that she is the first redeemed."[35] It is therefore possible to say that Mary is not only the perfect icon of the Incarnation, but also the *perfect icon of our own transformed life*, of the life of heaven that we are called to live out already here on earth.

She is the first to have known God as fully as it is possible for a creature to know him, as we too shall know him in heaven. She knew him not in her head — she did not *understand* any more than we do — but in her heart. (Luke 2:19, 51) She embodied him in her whole life, as well as in her "dormition," her death, and was the first to recognize Truth in the Person of her Son and offer it to the world.

Truth Is a Person

On the eve of his death, as if foreseeing the question *What is truth?*, which Pilate would ask him a few hours later, Christ told his disciples that he, Christ, was the Way, the Truth and the Life. (John 14:6) Those who knew him already knew the Father and the way to eternal life. Thus, in the clearest possible words, the Gospel proclaims that the way to Truth is a *relationship* between us and the Person of Christ and, through him, God.

When this immense mystery begins to penetrate our minds and hearts, our perspective on who God is must radically change. If Truth is not, as we usually understand it, a body of knowledge or belief but a Person, a Life, we begin to realize more clearly than ever before that we cannot work it out as we work out a problem or a puzzle. We cannot study it as we study science or logic. Rather, we encounter it in the Person of Christ, in whom we recognize the ultimate Icon of God and in whom we place all our faith.

We learn who God is from him as quickly or as slowly as we are able. We learn by living rather than studying. We learn by attending to him, by "abiding" in his presence and above all by doing what he has commanded us to do: by loving. To learn the Truth that is a Person takes a lifetime of discipleship, of learning to love.

This is also true, I believe, although also in a radically, "unambiguously" human way, of all the holy men and women who have ever lived. They, too, are bearers and icons of God. We learn the Truth from them by watching them, living with them and experiencing their love. They are the clearest signs, the mirrors, reflecting the Mystery of God made flesh, of the Invisible made visible, the Infinite putting on the finite. They teach us the deepest meaning of the Communion of Saints.

Here, finally, at least for me, is the answer to the question we asked at the beginning of these reflections. Although this answer may not satisfy a Zen master, although it may not banish forever the doubts that so often assail my own constantly thinking and checking mind, my heart knows that it is true. God is the One whom we meet and recognize in the Person of Christ; God is the Truth that burns at the core of reality and summons every human being into his presence.

He is the same Truth who called Moses in the desert and now comes to us from the pages of the Gospels, who makes himself present to us in the sacraments, whose face looks at us from the icons. He reveals himself to us in the teaching and prayers of the Church, in the lives of the saints, in the silence beyond all thinking and words. He may also come to us in the face of someone we love, in the cry of a child, in the touch of someone's hand. Sometimes we recognize him in the call of a bird, in the glory of the midnight sky, in a great work of art. He comes to us always in moments of suffering; he walks before us when we are bowed down and staggering under the weight of grief or pain.

Above all, he is the same Truth—the Christ within—whom we encounter in our hearts, in our deepest awareness of the mystery of God living in us and changing us into himself. God is always present, always the same, closer to us than our very lives—the Divine Wisdom who is also Love.

Priceless Gift

According to the Gospel of St. Mark, when Jesus and his disciples came to Bethsaida, "they brought to him a blind man and begged him to touch him." Jesus took the blind man away from the others and, "putting spittle on his eyes he laid his hands on him and asked, 'Do you see anything?' Looking up, he replied, '*I see people looking like trees and walking.*' Then, Jesus laid hands on the man's eyes again and he saw clearly." (Mark 8:22-25)

It was only recently, while rereading a poem my brother wrote many years ago, that I grasped the profound significance of this Gospel story. The poem places us in the position of the blind man when he is only half-healed: when he sees men "as if trees walking," when his vision is still unclear, distorted, meaningless. He is disturbed, uncertain of what to expect. What if he were to remain in that situation for the rest of his life? What if he were always only to half-see, half-understand? What if all he could ever say about the Mystery that had touched him that day were to remain as inadequate, as unclear as "the trilling of a bird that cannot sing"? He realizes that there is nothing he can do by himself; he can only wait. And so, the poem concludes:

I must wait for his second touch
And if he never does? Even that is well.
Half a sight is a priceless gift
God also loves what is incomplete.
May His name be praised!
May His name be praised.[36]

Very few of us are given the fullness of sight in
this life. The prophets, the great mystics, some of
the saints are the ones who are given the power
of the Spirit and sent to proclaim the Truth to the
world. Most of us, however, are not called to such
a high task. We must love God and do what he asks
of us without knowing very much, without seeing
very clearly, only half-believing, perhaps. But, if we
realize what a great grace it is to be able even to
half-see, to half-know, to half-tell, we too shall praise
him for his "priceless gift." We shall praise him for
having touched us at all, for letting us meet him on
the way.

There shall always be times when our half-
knowing weighs heavily upon us, when it appears to
us not as a vision of faith but as the darkness of doubt
and disbelief that threatens to engulf us. We may feel
close to despair and imagine ourselves irretrievably
lost. We may conclude that we have been deceiving
ourselves, chasing an illusion, an irrational dream;
that we have been like frightened children telling
ourselves fairytales in the dark. We may turn away in

a paroxysm of anger and self-contempt. For a while we may feel relieved, liberated: free at last to return to a more reasonable path, to reclaim our right to search for wisdom in our own human way.

Yet, once we have been given a glimpse of the reality of God, we can never quite let go of it, forget or deny it, even if we may sometimes feel we are close to doing so. God has imprinted himself on our hearts; we bear his image. He has made himself present to us. For this reason, in a way we can never comprehend, our hearts—our true minds—are capable of recognizing God when we encounter him in our own human reality, in our own human flesh. We can embrace him—and *live* his life by love until one day all is consummated in the reality of heaven and we at last, as St. Paul tells us, shall know him as we are known. (1 Corinthians 13:12)

Notes

1. Rudolf Otto, *The Idea of the Holy* (Oxford: Oxford University Press, 1990).
2. This does not mean that every story of "mystery" or fantasy is good for children and awakens them to the real sense of mystery on which faith can be built. Parents need to be alert and protect their children from those who, for the sake of celebrity or gain, may abuse or distort children's natural attraction to mystery.
3. It has most often been interpreted to mean "I am who I am," thus revealing God as "pure Being": eternal, unlimited and absolute. It was interpreted in this way by St. Thomas Aquinas in the thirteenth century; this interpretation became the cornerstone of Catholic Western theology, at least until recent times. But YHWH can also be understood to mean "I am he who causes all things to be," i.e., Creator of all that has come to be, a reading of the Hebrew favoured by many modern biblical scholars. See the appropriate sections of the *Jerome Biblical Commentary*.
4. Quoted in Bishop Kallistos Ware, *The Orthodox Way* (Crestwood, NY: St. Vladimir's Seminary Press, 1996), 12.
5. Ibid., 14.
6. Mother Maria Gysi, *The Fool*. Library of Orthodox Thinking (Normanby, Whitby, North Yorkshire, UK: Monastery of the Assumption, 1980), 58. Mother Maria was an Orthodox nun, the foundress and Abbess of the above Monastery, where she died in 1977.

7. St. Augustine, quoted in the *Catechism of the Catholic Church,* no. 158.

8. St. Anselm, ibid., no. 141.

9. *The Cloud of Unknowing,* trans. by Ira Progoff (New York: Dell Publishing Co., 1983), 72. Emphasis added.

10. *Sayings of the Desert Fathers,* trans. by Benedicta Ward (London: Mowbray, 1981), 68.

11. In Bishop Kallistos Ware, *op. cit.,* 133.

12. Catherine Doherty was the foundress of Madonna House Lay Apostolate in Combermere, Ontario, Canada.

13. *Sayings of the Desert Fathers,* 4.

14. Bishop Kallistos Ware, *op. cit.,* 138.

15. It is possible to say that grace — in whatever form or whatever "channel" it comes to us — is always the gift of living in God's *presence.* It may be of interest to note that it was used in that sense with reference to royalty in medieval times, when "Your Grace" was the normal way of addressing a king or queen. To be in the "King's grace" meant to be admitted to his presence and thus, to be able to present one's case "to his face."

16. St. Augustine, *The Confessions,* Book VI, 1 (New York: Doubleday Image, 1960), 133.

17. Quoted in St. Thomas Aquinas, *De Veritate,* questio 1. Cf. also *Catechism of the Catholic Church,* nos. 846-848.

18. *Catechism of the Catholic Church,* no. 170.

19. As an Orthodox priest pointed out to me recently, in the ancient Church, "dogmas" did not attempt to define the truth that was indefinable, but rather to define or explain what was *not* true: the errors and heresies that plagued the early Church. In other words, in order to know what is true, we must understand and let go of what is not true.

20. The significance of "Don't know!" was certainly not absent from the Christian West. In *The Cloud of Unknowing,* for example, we find this statement: "But now, you put

a question to me asking, 'How shall I think about him, and what is he?' And to this, I can only answer, 'I do not know.'" *op. cit.*, 72.

21. Cf. Shunrui Suzuki, *Zen Mind, Beginner's Mind,* ed. by Trudy Dixon (New York: Weatherhill, 1970).

22. St. Therese of Lisieux, *Story of a Soul*, trans. by John Clarke, OCD (Washington, DC: ICS Publications, 1976), 224.

23. Irma Zaleski, *Mother Macrina* (Ottawa: Novalis, 2000), 50–51.

24. *Practice of the Presence of God* by Brother Lawrence, Second Conversation. This little book is filled with similar references. There have been many editions of this classic work.

25. *The Cloud of Unknowing*, 133.

26. St. John of the Cross compares this "enlightenment" of the human soul to the removal of cataracts from the eyes that could see reality only dimly before. See *The Living Flame of Love* (Garden City, NY: Image Edition, 1962), 130.

27. Mother Maria Gysi, *The Fool*.

28. *On the Incarnation,* chapter 54.

29. The *Catechism of the Catholic Church* defines "grace" as "participation in the divine life" (no. 1997). Cf. 2 Peter 1:4.

30. *Living Flame of Love*, the first stanza, 32.

31. *Sayings of the Desert Fathers*, 103.

32. See I. de Beausobre, *Flame in the Snow* (Constable: London, 1945).

33. *Acathist*, Kontakion of the Annunciation.

34. Ibid.

35. Mother Maria Gysi, *The Fool*, 79.

36. J. A. Ihnatowicz, "Book of Hours," trans. C. Zakrzewski (in preparation).